Powerful Prayers

G·K
Hall
&Cº

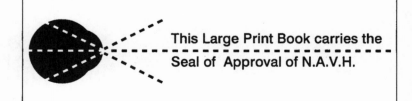

This Large Print Book carries the
Seal of Approval of N.A.V.H.

Powerful Prayers

LARRY KING
with Rabbi Irwin Katsof

WITHDRAWN

G.K. Hall & Co. • Thorndike, Maine

To Shawn —
the answer to my prayers

*Behold, how good and how pleasant it is
for brethren to dwell together in unity!*
— Psalms 133

Contents

Foreword 9
Author's Acknowledgments 11
Introduction 13

Chapter One   Prayer 101 19
Chapter Two   Prayer and the Preacher 38
Chapter Three   Prayer and the Artist . . 68
Chapter Four   Prayer and Our Leaders 102
Chapter Five   End of the Rope 119
Chapter Six   In Sickness and
                       in Health 153
Chapter Seven   Prayer and
                       the Big Deal 190
Chapter Eight   Prayer and Sports . . . 218
Chapter Nine   Prayer and Politics . . . 251
Chapter Ten   Prayer and War 276
Chapter Eleven   Everyday Prayers . . . 298

Epilogue 337
Afterword 341
Co-Author's Acknowledgments 343
Index 347

Foreword

As the founding pastor of the Crystal Cathedral Ministries many people know me as a prayerful man. At a very early age, I began to pray every night before I went to bed that God would make me a preacher when I grew up. That one prayer sustained me through my youth and it challenged me to grow to meet the requirements. Now, at the age of seventy-two, I can say that my first prayer was answered and is still being answered beyond my wildest expectations.

As a child, my friend Larry King dreamed of being a radio announcer — I understand his childhood nickname on the streets of Brooklyn was The Mouthpiece. Larry's dream, like my prayer, sustained and challenged him. I think he too would say that his dream has been fulfilled beyond his wildest expectations. Our stories share much in common. However, Larry does not think of himself as a prayerful man.

To me, prayer is an adventure into realms never before traveled, with an optimistic anticipation that there is something more out there, beyond what I already know or have already experienced. In this book, Larry has done exactly that — he has ventured into unknown territory:

the world of prayer. Armed only with questions, and his inimitable style, Larry set forth to interview powerful people on the subject of their prayers and he returned to write a book of amazing humor and insight.

Larry King has surveyed the divergent voices of America's spiritual renewal and has orchestrated them into "a joyful noise unto the Lord." From presidents and pranksters, friends and foes, believers and nonbelievers, Buddhists, Muslims, Jews, and Christians alike, *Powerful Prayers* is a symphony of faith and testimony.

It is my belief that we each connect to God in our own special way — be it through vision, a dream, or a hope. If we embrace that vision, nurture that dream, and lead an optimistic life in hope of an answer to our best desires, then we have tilled the ground in preparation for God's seed. As the son of an Iowa farmer, I can say that Larry has hoed a row.

And all things, whatsoever ye shall ask in prayer, believing, ye shall receive.
— Matthew 21:12

Dr. Robert H. Schuller

Acknowledgments

I am grateful to my daughter, Chaia, who, once again, opened up a world to me that I wouldn't have otherwise seen. My thanks to Pat Piper who worked with me in radio and helped me to write these words, and to Rabbi Irwin Katsof who lost twenty pounds teaching me about prayer but now knows the DH rule by heart.

Thanks to Marc Goldman of Damon Brooks Associates whose phone numbers and contacts made a difference in these pages; to my editor and copy editor, Joe McNeely and Ann Hartley, who offered guidance even the heavens couldn't give; and to my assistant, Judith Thomas, who finds the time in The Schedule for me to look out the window.

And my thanks to you, the reader, for allowing us to share our journey of the past year and a half with you. We hope these pages will become a part of your journey.

Introduction

During the past forty-plus years I've made a comfortable living having conversations with famous people. Being somewhat of an expert on talking, I am well aware that no conversation begins without a question of some kind, even something as banal as "What's happening?" or "How you doing?" As a kid growing up in Brooklyn, these questions would be the reason for an hour-long conversation on the neighborhood stoops. So how did I become interested in the prayers of powerful people? With a question, of course.

In early 1997 I was having dinner with my daughter, Chaia. Somewhere between the Caesar salad and the vegetable soup, she said, "You're always having conversations with powerful people, why not ask them about their prayers?"

Chaia has always been spiritual, a quality that sure didn't come from me. I'm agnostic, but to Chaia I've never preached — if I can use that word — that my view was the only view. As Chaia grew up she would talk to me from time to time about her belief in something bigger, a common denominator that connects us all. I encouraged her to follow that conviction and, in doing so, found myself wishing I shared her faith. My parents prayed, my wife, Shawn, prays and many of my close friends pray. Me? I don't know to what or to whom I'd be praying so I have always left it alone.

"Why don't you ask the powerful about their prayers?" she asked, to which I answered, "I'm not a preacher. I wouldn't know where to begin."

Chaia looked right through me, as only a daughter can, and said, "You interview lawyers and you're not an attorney, you interview Colin Powell and you've never been to war, and you interview Michael Jordan and you can't do a lay-up." She had a point.

I thought back to a year earlier when I ran into an old friend one morning in Los Angeles. It was a busy day. My schedule — The Schedule — was booked: nineteen meetings, two tapings of my CNN program, and an afternoon speech to some group about my career in journalism. Other than that, I had nothing going on.

My friend was working for the Jerusalem Fund of Aish HaTorah, an international educational organization dedicated to awakening the Jewish people to the power and beauty of their thirty-five-hundred-year heritage. My friend was looking for a celebrity to headline their telethon. I was familiar with the Jerusalem Fund and had approved the use of my name for their fund-raising efforts, but I was too busy to get more involved. The Schedule said it couldn't be done, but as a favor to my friend I agreed to meet with Rabbi Irwin Katsof, the executive vice-president of the Jerusalem Fund.

Ninety minutes later, the rabbi was in my hotel room. I really had no time to become more involved than lending my name and was ready to say so. I don't know why, but moments after meeting the rabbi I said, "How about I host this event, serve as chairman, and make some calls to see who else I can get involved?" It was the only time since I've known Irwin Katsof that he was at a loss for words. When he finally recovered, he said he had been trying to reach Sumner Redstone, chairman of Paramount Pictures, and couldn't.

Next thing I knew, I was on the phone talking to Sumner. He said he would be happy to help out and offered the use of a Paramount sound stage from which to do the broadcast — for free. In April of 1996, the Jerusalem Fund beamed a live fund-raiser to ten countries across four continents and collected some serious money to aid Soviet Jews. From that moment on, I was more than just a name on the Jerusalem Fund's letterhead.

Rabbi Katsof told me later that he had said a prayer in the elevator on the way up to my hotel room. He prayed that I would be open to his needs and he prayed for God's guidance; he had sweated over the details of this telethon for six months and I had gotten the job done in ten minutes. The rabbi devoutly believes that God answered his prayers that day. I don't recall any divine directive making me say what I said that morning, but say it I did and I suppose that's what counts.

When Chaia then proposed that I write a book on the prayers of powerful people, I was still uncertain, so I turned to the rabbi for assistance. No, let me put it this way: I called the rabbi for supervision. I knew absolutely nothing about prayer. Well, almost nothing.

I prayed during the 1949 World Series when the Brooklyn Dodgers faced their uptown rivals, the New York Yankees. That year, every Dodgers fan prayed for victory but we all discovered, much to our disappointment, that God was a Yankees fan — the Dodgers lost four games to one. The Yankees outplayed us and the Yankees fans outprayed us. I made the mistake of relating this story to Rabbi Katsof during our first meeting about the book in the dining room of the Plaza Hotel.

"Mr. King, God isn't a Las Vegas slot machine. You don't deposit a prayer in return for a payoff."

I was puzzled. "If you can't pray for a payoff, then why pray?" But I kept the thought to myself. Instead, I told the rabbi that he was about to embark on a long "road trip" with a spiritually challenged yahoo as his partner.

Rabbi Katsof's specialty is adult education

and I knew he couldn't pass up a challenging reclamation project like me. He was hooked. And I was hooked too. Curiosity has been the driving force in every interview I've ever done, and even though I don't sign my name to God's starting roster, I was suddenly curious about powerful people who do.

I look at it this way: the rabbi knows a lot about prayer, but I know baseball. Growing up in Brooklyn, baseball is real life — meat and potatoes — and everything else is parsley. I love to use the national pastime as an analogy. For example, people think catchers are dumb, but they're the smartest players on the field because they see everything. So that was my plan — be the catcher, sit back on my haunches, get a feel for the game, and scope out this prayer thing.

If I could get the rabbi to give me an insight into what I'm told is the most powerful conversation of all, then I could save myself from having to leg-out a lot of weak grounders. Road trips can wear you out if you don't pace yourself.

After hundreds of interviews, thousands of pages of transcriptions and handwritten notes, too many stories ripped out of newspapers and magazines, scores of late night and early morning phone calls with the rabbi, the road trip is over. Many of the powerful were eager to talk about their conversations with God. A few told us they've never talked with the Most Powerful of All and still others said the topic was too personal.

What follows is a revealing look at intimate thoughts, private moments, and powerful prayers. I know I came back from the road trip wondering if this older man, on the edge of a new millennium, now has a better understanding of why that young boy in the fifty-cent seats at Ebbets Field thought prayer was his final refuge.

This conversation begins as everything in my life begins — with a question: What is prayer?

Rabbi Irwin Katsof and I were in my New York hotel room.

I mentioned all the people I had seen at the Western Wall in Jerusalem with bowed heads and folded hands and how they differed from Catholics who genuflect and do the sign of the cross. Then I brought up the early Sunday morning religious services on television, with people throwing their hands in the air, singing out "Amen" or "That's right — praise Jesus" while the preacher is delivering the sermon. Could one of them be right and the rest of them wrong? So my first question to the rabbi was, "Is there a correct way to pray?"

"Mr. King," he began (I'd soon learn that whenever the rabbi addressed me as Mr. King, he was about to take me to school — I was the student and he was the teacher), "if there was only one way to pray, then we would all be Jews, or Muslims, Buddhists, Baptists, Catholics, or Mormons. I can keep going, but I think you get my point."

Rabbi Katsof pointed out the window, down to Central Park South where hundreds of

19

people were in motion. "Look out there. Right now, someone on the street is saying a prayer, just as right now I am saying a prayer. Different people, different places, different prayers — each with the same destination."

I was quiet for a second, not an easy task for me, but I thought: I've always gone with my gut feeling and my gut was telling me to ask the question. So I did. "You're saying a prayer right now?"

The rabbi looked at me with an expression that might have implied, "God, am I being tested here?" Then he continued patiently, "Yes, I'm talking to you, but during this discussion I've prayed that we will be guided on this project. However, prayer alone doesn't do the work. That's up to us."

I looked out the window to see if I could find the person praying. It seemed like a good place to start. There was a lady in a blue suit wrapping a scarf around her neck as she crossed Central Park South against the light. Was she praying not to get hit by a cab? Was it the construction guy sipping coffee? Or the man on the cell phone? Was he praying the shares in his company would go up? From the twenty-fourth floor it was anybody's guess.

The rabbi continued. "Everyone has a different way of connecting to God. We have different beliefs, we speak different languages, and we use different words. But if there is any rule at all concerning prayer, it is that however you pray you must be willing to put forth an effort for your prayer to be answered. Let me tell you a story . . ."

I have always been wary of people who preface their stories with "Let me tell you a story" because it can often be as long as a Senate filibuster. But before I could beg off by saying that I had to go to the bathroom or work on a cure for the Epstein-Barr virus, he began.

"It's a short story. The Jewish people are fleeing Egypt and they come to the . . ."

"Red Sea," I quickly filled in. I may not be very religious, but I've been to enough Passover seders to know that the Book of Exodus is not such a short story.

"The Jews are trapped on the shore and the Egyptian army is getting closer. The Jews have nowhere else to go but into the water. Everyone is in a panic. But there's this one guy, Nachshon Ben Aminadav, who jumps into the Red Sea all the way up to his nose. The water is rising, and guess what happens?"

"Charlton Heston parts the Red Sea and the Jews are saved."

"It's Moses, Mr. King. But not even Moses — God parts the Red Sea. But that's not the point," the rabbi said. "The point is, you can't stand on the shore just praying, you have to jump in all the way. You have to be prepared to sweat, sometimes even to die. Otherwise, why should God work for you if you won't work for yourself? God doesn't want to hear noise. He wants to see your effort."

Rabbi Katsof looked at me and smiled. "See? I told you it was a short story."

I've got an even shorter one. What's the synopsis of Passover and every other Jewish holiday? They tried to kill us. We won. Now, let's eat.

> **Prayer should be the key of the morning and the lock of the night.**
> — OWEN FELLTHAM, *RESOLVES* (1620)

AS THE sun rises to reveal the breathtaking beauty of the Hudson River and the mountains in upstate New York, the morning light streams through the window to awaken Pete Seeger. He is almost eighty now and though he no longer drags his banjo around the world as he used to do with his band, The Weavers, he still loves a song and a story.

He used both to talk with me about prayer.

You know, I greatly admired Mahalia Jackson, the great gospel singer. Once, when she was in the hospital, Studs Terkel and I stopped in to visit her. She talked about a song she used to sing, "I've seen God — I've seen the sunrise." If I can use the word here, it dawned on me, that's it! And I've said, since that time, "I'm with you, Mahalia." I wrote a song about it, as a matter of fact.

I was out to get some firewood one morn-

ing to warm the house and I saw the sun coming up. I thought to myself, "Dear God, I really hope we manage to survive all these problems we've created for ourselves."

Early in the morning I first see the sun,
I say a little prayer for the world.
I hope my little children live a long,
    long time,
yes, every little boy and little girl.
I hope they learn to laugh at the way
    our precious
old words seem to change,
'Cause that's what life is all about:
    to arrange and
re-arrange and re-arrange.
              — PETE SEEGER,
    "ARRANGE AND RE-ARRANGE"

I remember my father saying to me, "We live in a lingo-centric predicament." That means the world is just filled with people using words and thinking they know the definition. I mistrust words. If the world fails to survive it may be because of an over-dependence on words.

My prayer in the morning is "What next?" I think prayer can be for yourself, but it should be for everyone. We need to think about the future and that means thinking about others.

DR. JOHN GRAY is best known for his *New York Times* bestseller *Men Are from Mars, Women Are from Venus*. Many social observers cite the popularity of books about getting along with other people as concrete proof that American society is searching for something more meaningful than just me, me, me. Prayer appears to be a fundamental tool in that search as over eighty-five percent of all Americans claim that they pray. You can include Gray, who spent seven years as a monk before becoming America's number-one expert on the differences between men and women.

I pray every night before I go to bed and every morning. It is a conversation. There are four components in my prayer. First, I share any apprehensions. Second, I get in touch with what I want. This is my soul speaking, so it's not an I-want-a-new-BMW kind of thing — it's more than that. I want to be the best I can be and I want to help people. Third, I put out statements that are charged with positive feelings, full of purpose. And I imagine them actually happening and how that would feel.

Fourth, I say thank you. If we don't appreciate what we have now, then I don't think God will give us more. If you can release negativity, get in touch with what you want and then ask for it from the heart, it will work. The door will open and faith is imagining it is going to happen.

Lou Holtz, former coach of the Fighting Irish, winner of one hundred football games in ten seasons at Notre Dame — God's football team — told the rabbi and me that he uses the acronym ACTS as the playbook for his prayers.

My wife and I try to pray together in the morning. We say a prayer out loud expressing our thoughts, then we'll read Psalms from the Bible, or Proverbs, and I have a book with a prayer for every day with different passages from the Bible. I use the word ACTS: Acknowledge God, Confess what has happened — I lay it all on the table, so to speak — Thanksgiving for daily things, and then Supplication, which is whatever your needs and concerns are.

I've done this for quite a few years. I also try to pray during the day, just short prayers, maybe even a line or two, just a few words. It's a reminder to me that God is there.

Prayer, to me, is nothing more than talking to God and explaining how you feel and asking for his guidance. But prayer will seem hollow if you haven't a closeness to God. If you don't feel that closeness it's because there is something that is a barrier within you; maybe it's something you've done or a habit in your life which prevents you from having this relationship. God will tell you what to change, but you have to be sincere. Beginners in prayer have to get on their knees and tell God they can't lead their lives without him.

You'll have peace and satisfaction – you can handle the good and the bad – it just makes all the difference in the world in the way you approach life. You can be a Muslim, Jew, whatever. It doesn't matter.

If you feel distant from God, remember it isn't God that moved.

— ANONYMOUS

RABBI KATSOF and I were again in my New York hotel room and I said that I felt like the odd man out. Everyone was talking about where and when and how they prayed and I just wasn't getting it. Maybe it's because I don't do it, but it was like these people were talking Swahili.

"I understand everyone has a different way of praying, I just don't get the part about praying in the first place."

That brought the conversation to an abrupt halt for a full minute. And when it's just you and another guy in a quiet room, a minute can feel like an hour.

Finally, the rabbi spoke, "Let's go back to the beginning. Let's talk a language you understand: How would *USA Today* approach this?"

He pulled out a pencil. "We're going to make a list just like the one they print every morning on the front page of *USA Today*, below

26

the fold, left corner.

"You know, I write a column for *USA Today.*"

"Why do you think I'm suggesting it," the rabbi replied. "There are four things you must keep in mind about prayer. First of all, prayer is easy and prayer is difficult."

"How can it be both?"

The rabbi's hand went into the air. "Please, this is going to make sense. It is easy because prayer is a conversation. It is difficult because prayer requires that you pay attention to your words and thoughts. In a crisis, a sincere prayer can transform your life, if you are focused, if you are intent on the words and thoughts." With that the rabbi wrote "Prayer is easy and difficult" next to the number one.

"Second, prayer is an instrument for change. You will be different after making a request, from the person you were before. But remember this, what you think is best for you may not be what God knows you need." He wrote it on the paper, "Number two: Prayer should change you."

"Third, prayer connects you to your inner self. Prayer is for you, not for God. Look at the experiences you have in life — each presents you with an opportunity for another prayer, another chance to feed your soul."

The rabbi stood at the window and pointed outside. "Prayer helps you not only learn about what's out there, but in here as well," and he pointed to his heart. Then he wrote, "Number three: Prayer connects you to your true self."

"Last of all, prayer is a way to talk to the Master of the Universe, the Creator, the Almighty. It allows you to go right to the source." He wrote, "Number four: Prayer goes to the source," and handed me the sheet of paper.

I looked at it and nodded.

"So what do you think?" the rabbi asked.

"Makes sense," I said, putting the paper in my back pocket. "Of course, just because it makes sense doesn't mean I buy into it."

Rabbi Irwin Katsof leaned forward in his chair. I was in for it. I just knew I was in for it.

"Let me tell you a short story," he began. Another short story? For a moment, I considered faking a seizure and being rushed to a hospital before he could get started, but I was too late and he was on his way.

"In 1972, Dr. Abraham Twerski started the Gateway Program at St. Francis Hospital in Pittsburgh. It's an AA program to help people addicted to alcohol. The first three steps of the twelve-step program are for the alcoholic to admit he is powerless over his addiction, come to believe that a power greater than himself can restore him to sanity, and turn his will and his life over to the care of God. This is key. Once an alcoholic realizes he's in trouble, he tries anything to control his drinking, but ultimately nothing works.

"The alcoholic then realizes that he cannot do it alone. So, if he's not going to die from drinking, he's going to have to enlist some power greater than his own. He entreats God to help him complete what he cannot do alone. The alcoholic accepts powerlessness in the face of the addiction and submits to a higher authority."

"So?"

"Dr. Twerski told me about one alcoholic who doesn't believe in God and saw no reason to pray. It was a waste of time."

"That's what I'm saying."

"So the guy says the heck with it and walks out."

"Makes sense to me."

"A few months later, the guy comes back to the program. He pleads with his sponsor to help him with his drinking problem. He says he can't quit by himself and he'll do everything but the prayer part. So his sponsor tells him, 'Nobody ever said you had to pray to God. Just pray.' The guy thinks this through for a moment and decides he really doesn't have much choice. He starts praying. He's doing it to this day and he still doesn't believe in God. And, Larry, he is sober."

"That's crazy," I said to Rabbi Katsof. "He doesn't believe in God, but he prays? Who is he praying to?"

"Good question. Perhaps when the man prays, even if it is to no one in particular, he realizes *he* is not God, that he cannot control everything. He is admitting his own humanity and limitations — a very healthy thing to do."

I walked Irwin Katsof to the door, telling him how much I appreciated his help. I meant it. I can talk to a lot of people about a lot of topics, but this was tough. My catcher's knees were hurting and it was still only the top of the first inning.

> **HAROLD: Maude, do you pray?**
> **MAUDE: Pray? No, I communicate.**
> — HAROLD AND MAUDE (1971)

JEANE KIRKPATRICK was United States ambassador to the United Nations from 1981 until 1985, through some very tough times in the Reagan administration. She went head-to-head with the Soviet Union over the downing of a Korean Airlines jumbo jet that killed two hundred and sixty-nine people in September of 1983. She has this advice for anyone giving thought to having a conversation with God:

Just do it. That is exactly my advice. There was a time when I felt I didn't know any of the answers to the major questions — the Big Questions. And so I didn't do anything or say anything. I didn't attend religious services and I didn't say prayers. I just kept saying I can't do this because I don't know what it's all about. But after a while I realized I felt better when I honored religious observances. And I began to pray. And maybe because I grew older and expected less, it works for me now.

I think it's useful to begin prayer by thinking how much one has to be grateful for. How many blessings we enjoy, especially we Americans. We have so many of the good things that human beings through history didn't. So I think it's useful to begin with gratitude. I've never talked about this in my life.

I always pray some at night and in the morning when I wake up, and spontaneously throughout the day. I try very hard not to pray for myself. I say prayers alone and it becomes a way of focusing on where I am and what I should do. I pray for peace in the world and internal peace. I pray that I simply understand something better than I do. I pray that I can understand God's purpose in the world — not just for me but for all of us.

FLORENCE HENDERSON tells a story about saying a prayer to be on *Larry King Live*. Guess what? After her appearance I decided to talk with the actress who is known to America as Mrs. Brady, the ever-patient mother of *The Brady Bunch*. Florence was raised Irish Catholic and taught by Benedictine nuns. She says her work is her prayer. She even prays on the treadmill.

It's dedicating your day to God and, good or bad, whatever comes — accept it. My advice is if you haven't tried to pray, you should. And another important thing I think people should know is you don't have to be in a church or mosque or synagogue to pray. Prayer is with you all the time — it's your best friend. You're never really alone. The more you practice it, the easier it becomes.

To this day, I carry a book given to me by an actress when I was in The Sound of Music *called* Daily Strength for Daily Needs, *and I've had it recopied numerous times over the years. It's a prayer for every day of the entire year. Some of the prayers are hundreds of years old. I've learned that problems don't really change so much in life. We change. I can read the same prayer a year later and find I have a slightly different perspective on it. So if you keep your eyes open, you'll find all kinds of prayers in the strangest of places.*

DAVID SACKS is co-executive producer of the NBC series *3rd Rock from the Sun*. David prays three times a day and goes to shul (Yiddish for synagogue).

Some people have a tremendously con-descending attitude about religious people and religion. They'll take pains not to use the word "crutch," but nonetheless that's what they have in mind. They'll say, "I think it's so nice that religion plays a role in your life" or "I think it's so great that it gives you comfort."

This is a fundamental misconception about what prayer is about, what God is about, what religion is about. It's not like a little baby aspirin — it is a concept and a vision of what the world is. When you understand that God created the world, that God is running the world, there is no distinction between anything and God.

When you understand that, then prayer is an obligation and a necessity. If you're inhabiting the same world as God, how can you NOT want to talk to him? Let me give you an example. Imagine someone is married for twenty-five years:

So you live in the same house with your wife?

ANSWER: Yes, I do.

How's your relationship?

ANSWER: It's fantastic.

Do you ever talk with her?

ANSWER: Never.

Never? But you're very close?

ANSWER: Oh, incredibly close.

Now I ask you, what kind of sense does that make? You're inhabiting the same world with God. How can it be that you're not talking with him? God doesn't need anything from us, but he gives us the opportunity to connect with him through prayer.

> **Prayer for many is like a foreign land. When we go there, we go as tourists.**
> — ROBERT MCAFEE BROWN,
> INTRODUCTION TO JOHN B. COBURN'S
> *PRAYER AND PERSONAL RELIGION*

RABBI KATSOF and I were on the phone. He was in his office in Manhattan and I was . . . you know, now that I think about it, I don't know where I was. It was some hotel in the central time zone. That's all I remember, other than that ESPN was doing a piece about whether or not Pete Rose should get into the Baseball Hall of Fame. (The answer is he should, because if you want to mandate that all members have to be perfect human beings, then a lot of the current members ought to be tossed and that's never going to happen.) So my mind was a million miles away when the phone rang.

"So, what have you learned?" the rabbi asked.

"He deserves to be in the Hall."

"What hall?"

"The Hall of Fame . . . Cooperstown . . . baseball."

"What are you talking about?"

"Pete Rose."

"I must have missed something here. I was asking about prayer. You've talked to a number of people — do you understand it better now?"

"Oh." I turned down the volume on the television. "Well, I've learned that for some people it's a conversation, and sometimes it's a request. Sometimes it's just saying thanks and other times it's asking for strength."

"But it has to be the heart speaking, not just the mouth. And sometimes a prayer is just saying 'I want to be connected.' And sometimes it's an admission that you aren't the center of the universe."

"But I don't know if there is a God. I keep coming back to that."

"So pray anyway," Rabbi Katsof said. "Remember the alcoholic Dr. Twerski spoke of? Maybe you'll come up with an answer later."

"Suppose I was going to give it a shot. How would I start?"

"The first request in the formal Jewish prayer is asking for understanding. 'Help me to understand you. Show me the world has meaning.' But this can't happen unless you open your eyes. You have a role to play as well. Have you tried praying? Have you tried asking for understanding?"

"Here we go again, Rabbi. Who am I praying to? Who am I talking to?" I was getting frustrated. My question was being answered with a question.

"Larry, imagine you've come back from Circuit City with a brand new radio. You plug it in and all you hear is static. No music. No news. No baseball games. Do you call the radio stations and complain?"

"Of course not."

"Exactly. The signal isn't being received properly. You have to adjust the dial so it can pick up the radio waves. Same thing with God. He is there. He is on the air. You have to tune yourself to receive his signal, his bounty, and his blessing. But if your life is full of static — distractions, false ego . . ."

"I get it, Irwin. I'll give it some more thought, but I really better get going. I'm expecting a call from Judith, my personal assistant, to go over The Schedule. Then I have to be someplace. It's a long ride."

"Okay, Larry, but think about this. You're focused right now on having to be somewhere else. What about how you get there? That's important too. Larry, you need to have a relationship with God. Have a conversation, don't even call it a prayer. Just talking to God will be a good beginning."

"You're telling me to sit here and just start talking to someone I don't know from nothing about something I don't know anything about? Great conversation."

There was a long pause.

"Well, you're the one who said it's a conversation. You can't get a response if you don't talk."

"I promise, I'll think about it," I said as Pete Rose caught my eye again.

It was footage of Rose in the 1975 World Series which the Big Red Machine won four-three over Boston. Rose was Most Valuable Player. He was the 1963 National League Rookie of the Year. He played in 3,562 games, got on 5,752 total bases, and scored 2,165 runs. He was NL Batting Champ in 1968, 1969, and 1973, and his 4,256 hits broke Ty Cobb's record. What a man!

I was awakened from my statistical daydream by the insistent beeping of the fax machine. I walked to the desk and read the single page. It was from Judith, and it said, "Your line has been busy and we need to talk. NOW!" I went back to the sofa where I'd been sitting and found I hadn't hung up the phone. Irwin would love the symbolism of that. It was off the hook because I was so focused on Pete Rose. Who else wasn't getting through to me because I was too preoccupied?

Chapter Two
Prayer and the Preacher

On my television show, there are times when my producers will book an "expert" to explain an issue.

We don't do it very often because we prefer to interview the major player rather than those on the sidelines. I thought about this during another morning phone meeting with Rabbi Katsof. I said, "It's a shame we can't talk with the major player on this subject. If this were any other issue, I could be talking to the guy at the center of the story."

"God doesn't do interviews, Mr. King."

"And a big mistake, if you ask me. It would clear up a lot of my confusion. The problem is, Irwin, all I'm getting is a monologue. I'm looking for the dialogue, the other half of the conversation. On one side is the person saying the prayer and on the other side is the person listening — God — but he never talks back. That's not a conversation." I was starting to make some sense. My CNN crew would have been proud of me.

"God is talking, Larry, but you aren't paying

attention. The Almighty doesn't communicate like you and me. It's a different language. You have to slow down. God communicates to you through your wife, Shawn, your daughter, Chaia, your show. God uses you to communicate to others. There are no accidents."

"Me? God communicates through me? But I don't believe — why would he use me? Irwin, I'm getting frustrated. It's like that Nike slogan, 'Just do it.' Just do what? With whom? And most important, why?"

A very long pause. This was becoming a pattern whenever we talked. This pause was longer than your basic everyday pause. It was, in fact, an uncomfortable silence for me as I waited for the rabbi to respond. He didn't.

Silence is the finest of sounds.
— RABBI MENAHEM MENDEL
OF KOTZK

"Rabbi, hello? Are you still there?"

"I'm still here, Larry. I was just saying a prayer."

"Again?"

I don't get it. He just does it, goes into prayer mode with the snap of a finger or, in this case, at the first sign of an uncomfortable silence.

"I was asking God for wisdom and for patience because you can be very trying." I had heard that complaint before but nobody ever prayed about it.

I had a meeting coming up and three other phone calls to make, so we wrapped things up by agreeing to talk to some other experts.

"Larry, speaking as a rabbi who teaches and offers guidance, it is wonderful that you want to listen to other voices, get other points of view. In the end, it is your voice you must hear before you hear God's voice. I tell my students that all the time."

"I'll keep it in mind," I said as I hung up the phone. I sat for a few minutes thinking who I might know who would qualify as an expert on God. When I leaned over to get my little black book of phone numbers, it was already open to the name Thomas. I'm not one to believe in too many things — the rabbi will attest to that — but I decided my other business could wait while I called my good friend Cal Thomas.

Christians often ask why God does not speak to them, as he is believed to have done in former days. When I hear such questions, it always makes me think of the rabbi who was asked how it could be that God often showed himself to people in the olden days while nowadays nobody ever sees him. The rabbi replied: "Nowadays there is no longer anybody who can bow low enough."

— CARL JUNG
MAN AND HIS SYMBOLS

CAL THOMAS has one of the sharpest minds in Washington (okay, I can hear your guffaws about oxymorons), even though we disagree on just about every issue. The aisle between us is clear and sometimes wide, but I always learn something when he appears on *Larry King Live* to tell me how wonderful the Contract with America *could* have been.

When he worked on *Crossfire*, which was done live just down the hall from my set, there were many times when I walked past the studio and heard him arguing on the other side of the door. And they weren't even on the air. Cal writes a newspaper column, syndicated in over 450 newspapers across America, and he's a political pundit for Fox Television.

When I called him and told him the topic of my new book, there was a long pause on the other end — what is this thing with prayer and long pauses? — and then Cal Thomas offered this advice: "If you want to pray, Larry, you've got to know what number to dial."

How do you begin a conversation with God?

The first step in contacting God is to know how to reach him. If I want to know Larry King, I can ask your friends; I can read books by or about you. But to really know you, I must spend time with you. And, of course, as the Bible says, I must first acknowledge that you exist. That's why an agnostic never moves from his position. Though he says he's not sure if God exists, he is unwilling to find out by receiving information and asking questions.

I begin with God defining himself and listen for what he has to say to me. Some prayer is silent, but it's never — or should never be — one-way. God speaks to me through his spirit and through his words, the Bible, and even through others who know him, on occasion. He speaks certain general truths that are true for all time. And he speaks certain specifics that are true for me in my life at this moment.

Most people have ideas about God without ever having read his book or conversing much with him. You, Larry, are a conversationalist. So is God.

How does one reach God?

It's similar to the way I reach you, Larry. I have to go through someone — call the number and ask to speak to you. God, who is holy, allows access through his Son, Jesus, who makes those who receive him holy in his Father's eyes.

Cal, I'm Jewish.

So was Jesus.

Do you have a routine for prayer?

Yes, every morning I get up and go into the living room and pick up a book by Oswald Chambers and read a few verses and then I just start talking to God. My wife and I read the Bible together at night just before we go to bed, hopefully before the Leno monologue.

42

Oswald Chambers was a Bible teacher at the YMCA in Cairo, Egypt. After his death in 1917, Chambers' wife compiled his lessons in a book called *My Utmost for His Highest*. Cal recited one of his favorite passages to me.

Prayer is an effort of will. The great battle in private prayer is the swarming of mental wool-gathering. We must have a selected place for prayer and when we get there, the plague of the flies begins. This must be done and that is Shut Thy Door. A secret silence means shut the door deliberately on emotions and remember God.

JERRY FALWELL reads Oswald Chambers too. The Chancellor of Liberty University and founder of the Moral Majority goes into his study to pray every morning before breakfast, and before making any important decisions. Sometimes he needs twenty minutes, sometimes he needs an hour.

I pray first for my own needs — for wisdom, then for my family members by name and their particular needs as I know them, and for their protection. I pray for the ministry in which I'm involved and the people in it. After I got my computer I started building a to-do list every morning, with challenges and duties I must perform and things to pray about. I make changes in it every day and I try to get the right thoughts from the Lord about speeches I will give and television appearances. Prayer isn't just something I do in the morning — it's a life, not a posture.

Riding in the car is a good place to pray, while driving along the road alone. I believe vain repetition in prayer is unnecessary. God is not hard-of-hearing. God is not interested in your pain in your approach to him. God is not impressed with emotional exertions. God is a person, through his Son, Jesus Christ, and we can talk to him just as we talk to a person on earth.

It does not impress God when we shout or go through gyrations or when we sit and meditate for hours without a word. All those things are created by human beings. God is impressed with sincere hearts that approach him with simplicity.

It is human nature that draws people to prayer. We are creatures of need. Even the coldest heart finally comes to somewhere in life where there is nothing to do but call on God.

And for a man who is a media personality in his own right and host of the *Old Time Gospel Hour*, the Reverend Falwell had some words of caution for some of his televangelist brethren.

I watch programs with a videotaped prayer and someone says, "Put your hands on the screen for point of contact and I'll pray for your problem." That kind of thing bothers me.

It leaves the impression the person delivering the prayer is the answer and not to whom he is praying.

We have to be very careful and understand that prayer is a conversation with God and that can be intercession, petition, praise, or thanksgiving, and when change occurs it comes from God, not the person on the television. I don't believe in the point of contact and I don't believe in the preacher having unusual powers that extend beyond the layperson.

ISLAM HAS more than one billion followers. My next call was to Dr. Amir Ali, managing director of the Institute for Islamic Information and Education in Chicago, Illinois. I learned later, after we talked about prayer, that his doctorate degree was in biochemistry. No matter. Dr. Ali is an accomplished and intelligent advocate of the Muslim faith and a patient man. When the topic is prayer and I'm on the phone, patience is a requirement.

Dr. Ali started the conversation.

Did you pick being male?

No. I've never thought about it.

Did you pick being born a white man?

Same answer.

So, someone made the choice for you since you didn't make the choice yourself, right?

Beats me, Doctor. Maybe it just happened

that way and there wasn't any decision made. Maybe it was just happenstance.

You sure it was happenstance?

I've never thought about it.

So Dr. Ali walked me slowly through the Muslim approach to connecting with God or, in Islam, Allah.

The Islamic prayer removes people's sins. We tell a story about a group of people asking the prophet Muhammad why Muslims need to pray five times a day. The Prophet tells them, "If there is a stream at the door of one of you and you bathe five times a day, wouldn't it remove all the dirt from your body?" The group agrees it would and the Prophet says, "This is the likeness of the five prayers, with which God blots out all faults." We call this prayer Solat, and each takes about five minutes to complete.

We pray before sunrise, early afternoon, halfway between midafternoon and after sunset, at sunset until the redness in the sky is gone, and after dark before midnight. We pray facing Mecca, which here in Chicago is in the northeast. Look at it this way: We do a lot for our personal happiness through pur-chases and vacations and movies and so on, but we do very little for our spiritual happi-ness. We eat meals a few specified times a day and, in the same way, we pray at speci-fied times every day. It is a way to keep the soul nourished.

Dr. Ali said there are three kinds of Islamic prayer: (1) prescribed prayer, which is called Solat, (2) Dua, supplication, asking God (Allah) for something, and (3) Dhikr, reminding oneself of Allah all the time. All Muslim prayers fall into one of these three categories.

I thanked Dr. Ali for his time and was about to hang up when he said, "You know, of course, that prayer is natural to human beings."

I took a long pause and finally asked, "Natural?"

Mr. King, when the airplane is about to fall or the ship is about to sink, everyone prays — right?

I didn't answer. I paused again and Dr. Ali didn't wait for my answer.

Point taken?

I nodded in silence.

THE RABBI and I hadn't spoken on the phone for a while. I was doing my interviews, he was doing his interviews, but he kept in touch by littering my hotel room with faxes on prayer. Here's one of my favorites:

> **Prayer is compared to a bow:**
> **the more you stretch a bow,**
> **the more accurately it will score a**
> **   bull's eye**
> **and not miss the target;**
> **so too prayer:**

the more concentration and proper
intent a person adds to it,
the more it pierces the heavens and
breaks through the firmaments.
— *THE SAYINGS OF MENAHEM MENDEL*
OF KOTSK

RABBI MARVIN HIER is the founder of the Simon Wiesenthal Center, an international human rights organization that combats anti-Semitism. The Center is dedicated to preserving the memory of the Holocaust and teaching its significance to contemporary society.

Rabbi Hier is also a two-time Academy Award-winning producer, most recently for the documentary *The Long Way Home* about the struggle of the death camp survivors in the aftermath of World War II. The world is a better place as a result of Rabbi Hier's work. Here's a prayer I can endorse: "Never again."

Rabbi Hier offered me this advice: the best prayer never contains ego.

In the Jewish concept of prayer, God is identified by two names. We know him as Adonoi and Elohim. One of the twentieth century's greatest thinkers, Rabbi Joseph B. Soloveitchik, analyzed the difference between these names, saying Jews only pray to Adonoi and a Jewish prayer to Elohim is unheard of. This is because Elohim defines God as the creator of the cosmos, of the vast universe,

48

the creator of all the black holes out there, all of the universes beyond the black holes, and when we think of such a God, he's far from us. He is distant.

That is the God that man thinks of when man is in the mode of being a conqueror, when he goes about his daily chore of being a conqueror, successful in his career or trying to be successful in his career. When man looks at God from that vantage point, he'll always find him at the end of the galaxy.

To find the God named Adonoi you must be willing to be defeated, willing to surrender, to know you cannot be a conqueror all your life. You are mortal and a mortal human being must be defeated. A man must know how to say "I surrender" before an all-powerful creator. In that moment of defeat, when a man surrenders, he meets God not in the distant ends of the galaxy, but he meets God as a friend, as a confidant, as someone whose shoulder he can lean upon.

The only way you can have this relationship with God is if you approach him willing to be a defeated human being. If you approach God with total arrogance as if you're in charge of the universe — "I'm Mr. Everything, I'm the capital I" — the capital "I" will never meet God. He never appears to people with the capital "I." He only appears to those willing to be defeated, willing to be awestruck, willing to surrender before a greater force. To

49

them he appears as a friend and as a confidant.

Do prayers have to be formal?

I pray to God every day according to Jewish law. I remember once a person complaining about the ancient prayers. "It's so archaic, we're just mouthing things that have been repeated for generations. Of what significance is it, or relevance to our time, these ancient prayers?"

Rabbi Soloveitchik said that people often forget, and confuse the technique of prayer with the essence of prayer. The technique is only used to set up a mode so that the essence of prayer can take place. Imagine you are visiting somebody on a sickbed and the person is dying. Imagine it's a loved one. You exchange a glance. The glance is only a fleeting second. It is that eye contact that speaks a universal language, it is the essence of communication.

Likewise, when one prays, it's not the fact that the prayer has been set up in a whole series of pages that we turn — that's the technique. The essence of prayer is when you reach that right mode, that proper mode that every person knows, when you are ready to exchange a glance for a fleeting second between mortal man and the eternal. It is that fleeting second that is really the essence of prayer.

And I have experienced such fleeting sec-

onds, moments when I needed prayer and turned to God. For a fleeting second you feel as though you are overpowered by that sensation and that feeling. And then you know.

A great philosopher once said, "The difference between prayer and prophesy is that in prophesy God initiates the contact. And in prayer it is man that summons God, man initiates the contact."

IRWIN WAS sending me too many faxes so I decided to balance the equation and had Judith fax him this little snippet:

A rabbi and an alcoholic bus driver arrive in heaven at the very same moment. The rabbi is shocked when the bus driver is greeted with great accolades and immediately asked to come inside while the rabbi is told to wait outside for a moment. After a while the rabbi is brought inside and he immediately asks God why he had to wait after performing God's work on earth while the bus driver with the drinking problem was given a hero's welcome. God says, "Rabbi, when you spoke in synagogue everyone went to sleep. When the bus driver was on the job, everyone was praying."

51

SOME WOULD call Marianne Williamson a new age spiritualist. She thinks of herself as someone who teaches universal spirituality. We had an interesting conversation about her spiritual roots and her transformation into one of America's new spiritual pioneers. She is the author of three best-selling books — *A Return to Love, A Woman's Worth,* and *Illuminata* — and, most recently, *The Healing of America,* which explores the intersection of spirituality and politics.

What is your background?

I'm Jewish. In college, I was a student of comparative religion and philosophy, and I became very interested in a set of books called A Course in Miracles. *I don't know if you're familiar with it. It's not a religion, but a psychological training based on universal, spiritual themes. I started lecturing on the* Course in Miracles *in the early '80s. I wrote a book based on my lectures that published in 1992. From that point on, I've had an international career because I'm one of those lucky people whose book was liked by Oprah Winfrey.*

Was that the factor in making your books sell so well?

That first book, yes. It was before her book-of-the-month club. She was on her show and said, "I've never been so moved by a book. I bought a thousand copies. Everybody go buy it."

What was your background growing up as a

Jew? Did you have much religious education?

I was raised conservative, but I always told my mother I went to God in spite of my religious education. My work, as it's become well-known, is clearly nondenominational. I probably fill more churches than most ministers do. Many rabbis have called me into their studies and given me a dressing-down, and said, "You could have found it here." My response is, "You should have taught me."

I've said many times that if the mystical aspects of my own religion — the true, deep, spiritual truth of my religion — had been taught me, I'd probably be a rabbi today. But, it was not taught me.

Do you have a set time that you make sure you pray, or is it spontaneous?

I try to meditate once or twice a day, but my conscious contact with God is a never-ending conversation inside my head.

Are there any set words that you use?

When I meditate, I meditate either with a transcendental meditation mantra or with a sentence from A Course in Miracles. *In my regular prayer life, I simply talk to God and ask, on some level or another, for his help — asking that he correct my perceptions or show me what it is I need to see.*

Is there a specific incident in your life where you feel God answered your prayers?

There are so many. I feel that my whole life is a miracle. I was once, as so many people are, very unhappy, and now I have, while not always an easy life, a very meaningful life. I see his handiwork in that.

What makes your life meaningful now?

First of all, my daughter, because I don't think anything can compare to the experience of having that opportunity, but in terms of my work, I feel that I'm given — as an author, as a lecturer, and as a public figure — an extraordinary opportunity to serve.

Do you feel that God wants us to pray to him?

Oh, absolutely. Not only absolutely, but fervently! In A Course in Miracles it is said, "Prayer is the medium of miracles." I tell people often, to talk about God is different than talking to God.

Sometimes in my work I'll say to people, "Well, did you pray about it?" And sometimes they will say, "Oh, I know it's in God's hands." And I'll say, "That's not what I asked you. I didn't ask you if you know it's in God's hands. I asked you if you prayed."

To my understanding, to say that it's in God's hands means that ultimately things will work out to reflect God's will because God's will has never not been done. But that can take a very, very long time, since God will not counter your free will. To pray means to say "Dear God, as if your wish were mine," which opens up the universe to possibilities that did not exist before.

54

Some people say that prayer is a sign of weakness. How do you respond to that?

I respond to it the same way I respond to kindergartners who say ice cream is good food. To say prayer is a sign of weakness is to posit that the mortal mind knows more than the Creator of the Universe. And what can you say about such a silly thought?

I'm asking you.

It's laughable. Except, unfortunately, the state of the world is such that I have to say it would be funny if it were not so sad. We could literally pray away the problems of the world.

What do you mean by that?

If more people prayed, we would interrupt the flow of history.

If more people prayed?

Yes, if more people would pray, more consistently, we could literally, through the power of our prayers, lift the clouds of darkness that envelop the planet. It would wake us up to our essential nature and we would become our more noble selves.

That's a pretty powerful statement.

In the Star of David, as well as the Christian cross, there is a pictorial representation at the intersection of God's mind and our minds. The pyramid pointing to heaven intersects the pyramid pointing to earth. The horizontal axis of the earth intersects the vertical axis of God. That intersection point is the meaning of religion.

55

The word "religio" . . . the root is "to bind back." That, to me, is religion. The experience of going home to the Father while on the earth. That is what prayer does!

In your books, how do you teach people to pray?

I wouldn't say I teach people to pray. I certainly have suggestions in there and I say, you know, the point is not what words you use. I think people need to be reminded to pray, but people don't need to be taught to pray, not really. They think they do, but once they get into it there's a torrent of emotion behind this dam created by our over-secularized culture.

I meant it when I said to my mother that I went to God in spite of my religious education. I don't remember even a conversation when I was in Sunday school about prayer or about talking to God. I know so many people who are at this point embracing God in spite of their introduction to him as children. I was never turned off to Judaism, I just was never invited in the room deep enough to know the fruits that were there. I know they're there now.

How do you think prayer works?

I think that we have free will. And, therefore, our minds do not have to be with him. When our minds are with him, he literally lifts us to celestial realms. And the Red Sea parts if it has to part. Once our minds are with God, the universe literally opens up to us. But, most of us live in a state where our minds are closed to him. We're off doing it by ourselves. We're interfering with his plans by putting our plans before his. And that's because people aren't aware that his plan is a blessing for all living things.

A Christian Scientist little old lady friend of mine said to me once, "His plan blesses everyone and hurts no one." But many people are afraid to surrender to him. You don't know that surrender to him is freedom. But once you know that, you look at every problem in your life and you know the only reason you're having the problem is because his plan is not operative in your life. Then you can take responsibility, and that's where atonement happens — atonement is everything. Everything.

God scattered holy sparks all over the world. Whenever a person prays with intent, his words attract one of these sparks and propel it heavenward to add brilliance and sparkle to God's glorious crown.

— ARVEI NACHAL,
COMMENTARY ON THE TALMUD

ONE SATURDAY night after dinner in Greenwich Village, Shawn and I were in a cab returning to our hotel on Central Park South. The cabby had his radio tuned to WOR and we found ourselves listening to a Catholic priest, Father Paul Keenan. Usually, in a car I'm listening to Sinatra or Bobby Darin, but this cabby says he never misses the father's radio show. I turned to Shawn and said, "I must be spending too much time on this book."

Father Keenan works in the communications office of the Archdiocese of New York and his radio program is called *As You Think*. He's also just published his first book, entitled *Good News for Bad Days*. We hadn't interviewed a Catholic expert yet, so I gave Father Keenan a call. As it turned out, he was a fan. He had listened to my late-night radio show many years ago and he told me that I had been his inspiration for getting into radio.

I started by telling the father about my friend who never prayed before, but was now taking an interest in the idea. I asked Father Keenan what he could tell me about prayer so I could help my friend.

That wouldn't be you would it, Mr. King? I remember hearing you on the radio talking about being agnostic. I also remember the callers trying to tell you how to pray and how not to pray and who's right and who's wrong and who's going to hell.

You really were a listener.

Prayer is a relationship and I really think it happens when a lot of us get older. It isn't about finding someone who will do things for me or make my team win like some used to do back in the cheap seats of Ebbets Field when the Dodgers were playing in Brooklyn.

Every experience can teach us something about life and give us a sense of wisdom. We have bad days and we have to understand a bad day doesn't mean you are stuck in it forever. Bad days can teach us about life. And that's a wonderful time to pray and say, "Here is what is on my mind and help me to understand what I can get out of this." We like the idea that we are independent, we can run the show and have all the answers, and we are embarrassed when we realize that's not the way it works. So I understand your friend's reluctance to ask for help.

The first prayer is usually one asking for help. Just say, "God, I've never done this before and I'm scared and I don't know how to do it. But here's what's on my mind." When people say to me they don't know how to pray, I tell them that's okay — the way to learn it is to just start praying. All prayers are centered with why am I here, what is going on in my life, why are the things that are happening in my life happening, and if they're bad, does it have to stay this way? And then you ask for help.

The best prayer of all is to pray for the will of God. "You know better than I do, God, so I'm giving you the reins and I ask that you guide me and bring people into my life that I need to have."

IN APRIL 1997, the Dalai Lama was a guest on my show to talk about China's refusal to allow Tibetan self-rule.

After we covered the political issues and his upcoming meeting with President Clinton, the conversation turned to prayer.

What is the essential difference between Buddhism and other faiths?

Usually I describe it like this: Christianity, Judaism, and Muslim . . . these religions believe in a creator.

There is a creator?

Yes, there is a creator. Then there is Buddhism . . . that does not accept the concept of a creator.

What do you accept?

Self-creation. Something like self-creation. . . . Usually I describe godly religion and godless religion. This is the fundamental difference. However, I always look at the purpose of these different religious traditions. I feel they are the same. All are aiming at the betterment of the human being, trying to make a warm-hearted person, a sensible person . . . sensible humanity. All these major religions are talking about the importance of love, compassion, and the sense of forgiveness.

Do Buddhists pray? And if you pray, whom do you pray to?

Yes, we pray to Buddha — that means higher being.

Is Buddha God?

The Buddha — the origin of Buddha — is just like ourselves.

He was a man?

Yes, a man or sentient being, which is ordinary. Then, through his or her own practice, they eventually become enlightened. That we call Buddha, so we can consider them as a higher being . . . so they have an extra sort of energy and we can appeal to them in a form of prayer.

But your basic concept is belief in self?

That's right.

And love for others?

That's right.

After the interview the Dalai Lama, who is over sixty himself, slapped me on the back to thank me for the conversation. I can tell you, from firsthand experience, that he is strong. That slap stayed with me till the end of the program.

Dwell!
You are the Light itself
Rely on yourself
Do not rely on others
The Dharma is the Light
Rely on the Dharma

**Do not rely on anything other
than the Dharma**
        — MORNING SERVICE, SUTRA

THERE ARE nine senior teachers with Shambhala International, a group of Tibetan Buddhists. One of them is Judy Lief who lives in Yonkers. She has been a Buddhist since 1971 and lectures across America. She answered my questions about Buddhist prayer that I did not have time for with the Dalai Lama.

The first thing to understand about Buddhism is we don't worship an external God. We are part of everything else. God, or whatever name you choose, is inside. So our prayers aren't directed out toward something.

The first thing you have to do is simply learn to sit quietly. A Buddhist will meditate before praying. We call it uncovering your wisdom. It doesn't exist outside. It's inside. You have to calm the mind. If you can't do that, then I don't think it matters what version of prayer you want to use. It will take awhile. What you need is there, but it gets covered over and you get distracted and discursive and stuck in self-absorption.

Through the process of being quiet, you begin to note how your mind works and what arises in it, what and how you judge experiences. It's figuring out who you are. Who is it that's praying? Who is this person? Do I even know this person? Do we ever take the time, because we are rushing around, to actually stop and see each other?

So if you can clear your mind, the second step is to feel your heart — where are you closed in and where can you open further? The quality of prayer is that you have to be on the edge, pushing all the time just beyond the comfort zone, whether it's in the realm of awareness or compassion.

Beyond this, it is good to not have a strong boundary between what is formal prayer and your everyday life. Everything you do should have the quality of prayer. I think prayer is natural. There is a sense of the journey and we are all trying to figure it out. So I think it helps to have your heart broken a few times, failing at some things. It's like a rough pebble that gets tossed into the water and gets rounded down.

A Buddhist would never pray for himself or herself. For instance, if you aspire to be more effective or intelligent, is it motivated by con-tributing to the world or is it motivated by building your empire?

ROBERT SCHULLER is the founder of the Crystal Cathedral in Garden Grove, California. He is host of the long-running *Hour of Power* telecast every Sunday, which reaches more than a million viewers, and he has given spiritual counsel to a number of presidents.

Reverend Schuller got his start delivering Sunday morning sermons at a drive-in movie theatre — the concession was his lectern. He has been a frequent guest on my CNN show when the topic has turned to things spiritual.

Considering that he is the author of more than twenty books, one of which is titled *Prayer*, I knew Reverend Robert Schuller was someone I needed to talk to.

I was brought up on an Iowa farm. The first stage of planting is working the ground. You have to do that before you can plant a seed. It's the same way with prayer. There are lots of people having problems with prayer because the soil isn't good. People pollute the soil in their subconscious memory systems through hurt, rejections, bad relationships, so you have to remove the pollution. Prayer must have as its beginning positive thinking.

Here is a suggestion for somebody's first prayer: "Dear God. I don't know where to start. I'm going to try and talk to you. I don't know if I'm getting through. If I'm on the right track, let me hear you. And if I'm not on the right track, let me hear you."

Nothing is more important than honesty in prayer. There are no pretensions in prayer, so the best place to begin is wherever you are.

Before we hung up, Reverend Schuller offered this advice: The purpose of prayer is not to get what you want, but to become who you should be.

Practical prayer is harder on the soles of your shoes than on the knees of your trousers.
— AUSTIN O'MALLEY,
PROFESSOR OF ENGLISH AT
NOTRE DAME (1895–1902)

RABBI KATSOF and I arranged an early working breakfast to review our progress (read: my progress) on prayer. He came to my hotel room with a Diet Snapple, while I munched a bagel with a shmear of cream cheese and raspberry jelly, a hard-boiled egg, and coffee. As always, he was right on time.

"Irwin, I never see you eat," I said as I attacked my bagel. I gotta tell you, a bagel in New York tastes better than any bagel in Chicago or Des Moines or Los Angeles. I'm not sure why, but I suspect it must be the soft water in NYC.

"I keep suggesting we go to Kosher Delight," the rabbi said. "It's right around the corner on Avenue of the Americas. Then we both could eat. Did you read the fax I sent that quoted Rabbi Samson Raphael Hirsch?"

I nodded but the rabbi knew I hadn't.

"He lived in Germany during the nineteenth

century. He said, 'A tear is the sweat of the soul and the gates of heaven open before tears.' I think that's a wonderful definition. On the Jewish holy days of Rosh Hashanah and Yom Kippur I say prayers and, many times, find myself in tears. That's a good indicator a connection has been made. The soul has to be involved in the prayer. That's why I suggested that you must listen for your voice before you hear God's."

"Well, the experts told me, you got to take out the garbage first. That's where you begin."

Irwin choked on his Diet Snapple. "Garbage?"

"Well, I admit that's my interpretation. Cleanse yourself, free your mind, prepare the soil . . . something like that. I'm not one to repeat verbatim what I hear. I like to put it into my own words."

"You certainly do that. So, what comes after 'take out the garbage'?"

"I don't know. 'Put out the cat'? Anyway, I'm done with experts for a while. Experts are good, but that's 'cause they've studied it. I've got another idea. If the count is three-and-O, what do you do?"

The rabbi was puzzled as to where this was going and, to be honest, I wasn't so sure myself. "We're talking baseball again, right?"

"Of course we're talking baseball. Pay attention, this is important. You're at the plate. It's three balls and no strikes. The book says take the next ball. Statistically, you're going to draw a walk nine times out of ten. But I'm not going by the book because my gut tells me that pitcher thinks I'm not gonna swing, so he's gonna put a fast one down the chute. You're with me here, right?"

"All the way, Larry."

"I'm swinging for the fences . . . Y'know who we should talk to next? Actors."

"Actors?"

"Not just actors. Artists, singers, whatever. Art is supposed to interpret the world we live in, express how we feel about things — let's see what artists have to say about talking to God. Actors could be good."

"And they're already booked for your show?"

"Well, there's that too." Rabbis are a lot hipper these days than I remember.

"Okay."

"You're buying actors and artists?"

"Why not?" said the rabbi as he headed out the door. "God is the greatest artist of them all. He paints fabulous sunsets and creates birds that sing and everything else that's beautiful."

I was proud of myself. Prayer still didn't make sense to me, but what I was doing to understand it was starting to click.

Chapter Three
Prayer and the Artist

2:30 A.M.
I was wide awake in my
Los Angeles hotel
living room.

Maybe it was because I had traveled across three time zones twice within the past week, but that didn't matter right now. I had a full day scheduled ahead, a day with no time for a nap, much less even closing my eyes. I needed sleep and yet I was restless.

I picked up the TV remote in the hope that an old movie might induce me to relax. Then I thought of my wife, Shawn, asleep in the bedroom next door, and decided against it. It was bad enough one of us couldn't get any rest.

I decided to do some work instead. Irwin had sent me the transcript of his interview with Kirk Douglas, along with a copy of Kirk's book *Climbing the Mountain*. Between the books, the transcripts, and the faxes from the rabbi, I was going to have to rent a separate hotel room for storage.

I had been carrying the transcript with me for the past few weeks, and in this quiet moment I finally started leafing through it.

Although I was raised an Orthodox Jew, I went away from my religion and only redis-covered it late in life. Often I feel sad for the time I have lost and I feel resentful of the Jewish teachers of my childhood, who put such an emphasis on the form and funda-mentalism of the religion but not on the spiri-tuality. In my day, all the emphasis was on reading Hebrew but never on understanding it.

So a young Jewish boy like me could be filled with all kinds of rules that he never un-derstood, prayers that he never knew the meaning of, and it might take him years — like it took me — to begin to read translations of some of these prayers and realize the truth and beauty of what was being said.

The rabbi highlighted this portion of the transcript for me. In the margin it said, "Sound familiar?" All I knew was that Kirk Douglas was speaking from his heart and not mincing any words.

I picked up Kirk's book and read with inter-est as he spoke of his difficulties in reaching an accord with God:

I have had a tumultuous relationship with God, and he has let me know that he has not been so pleased with me — at least I think that this was the message when I began to experience severe back pain in my old age. C. S. Lewis, a Christian writer, said that "pain is God's megaphone to wake up a deaf world."

If that is true, then I was stone deaf. My wife kept telling me, "Don't read too much into it. The only thing God is telling you is that you are getting old." Maybe, but I thought otherwise.

And the rabbi highlighted this section of the book about Kirk's visit to the Western Wall:

I feel the place where God hears you better than anywhere else is the Western Wall, the Wailing Wall in Jerusalem. The last time I prayed there was in 1994. I remember it as if it were yesterday. The massive stones of the Wall were bathed in the golden rays of the setting sun. The plaza beneath the Wall was crowded with worshippers — praying the afternoon "Mincha" prayer. The energy emanating from all the praying Jews, davening at a wild pace was overwhelming.

I moved through the crowd. It was difficult to find a place to touch the Wall. I looked around for a crevice where I could put the tiny, folded-up piece of paper with my prayer. I found one. As I reached deep into it, my fingers touched other prayers placed there before me. I hoped that all those prayers had been answered.

It reminded me of the often told story of the blind, poor, childless man who prayed daily at the Wall that his fate might be reversed. And one day, during his fervent prayer, he heard the voice of God: "I'll answer your prayers. I'll give you one thing. What do you want most?"

The man was thrown into an emotional frenzy. What should he ask for? If he asked for sight, seeing his poverty would bring him grief. If he asked for wealth, what good would it be if he was still blind and had no children with whom to share his good fortune. But if he asked for children, how could he feed them being so poor, and besides it would break his heart not to be able to see them. Thus he agonized and finally he formulated this prayer:

"Dear God, grant me just one thing — the joy of seeing my children eating off of gold plates."

Only a Jew could come up with a prayer like that.

"Larry?" I was awakened by Shawn's hand on my shoulder. "It's 6:30. You have a breakfast meeting in forty-five minutes," she said. The last thing I remembered was reading Kirk Douglas's prayers. When had I fallen asleep?

I will solve my riddle with the harp.
— PSALMS 49:5

PETE SEEGER told us there are songs that are prayers.
I think, on stage, I'm part of a long chain of

71

people. When I'm singing I'm carrying on a tradition of people trying to survive in this world. I'm singing songs made up by other people, putting together melodies made up by other people, using words made up by other people, and playing instruments created by other people. All of those people are on stage with me.

One of my songs that became quite popular comes from the Book of Ecclesiastes. In 1959 I got a note from my publisher asking me if I could write something like "Goodnight Irene" instead of all the protest songs. I looked through a notebook I always carry with me and found some verses I'd copied down years earlier and added the lines "a time for peace, I swear it's not too late." That became "Turn, Turn, Turn" which The Byrds made famous.

> To everything (Turn, Turn, Turn)
> There is a season (Turn, Turn, Turn)
> And a time for every purpose under
>   heaven . . .
> A time to gain, a time to lose
> A time to rend, a time to sew
> A time to love, a time to hate
> A time for peace, I swear it's not
>   too late.
>   — FROM THE BOOK OF ECCLESIASTES
>   ADDITIONAL WORDS AND MUSIC
>   BY PETE SEEGER

DURING THE recording of "Turn, Turn, Turn" David Crosby, the singer and rhythm guitarist for The Byrds, gave little thought to the song other than it had nice chord progressions. That was in 1965. He was on the edge of what would soon become a twenty-year marathon with drugs and alcohol.

Today, more than ten years clean and sober, David Crosby told me he has a new perspective:

If you listen to "Turn, Turn, Turn" it is so eloquent. It is so right. Take it out of the religious context and it could be any religion. It is close to Buddhism. It says all things come around in a circle and it is almost like it's talking about karma. It's such a spiritual song.

I think Pete felt that way too, and he told me it rang his inner bell. It was a good song in the '60s and I liked what it said, but I didn't feel that it was a spiritual anthem. I do now.

WILLIE NELSON believes songs are prayers too. A self-proclaimed simple guy, this country-music legend says that he keeps his prayers simple too. The only prayer he uses is the Lord's Prayer.

Prayer has kept me from killing myself. You always ask for the strength in your prayers to keep you from doing dumb things, but you have to figure out what those dumb things are. A lot of times when you think you are asking God to do something, you are asking yourself to do it. God and yourself are not that far apart. He's already there. He knows what's going on. He knows what you are going to ask before you ask him. He knows what you want. He knows what you need. Prayer is more for you than it is for him.

I have a crisis every few minutes and prayer just seems like a safe place to be. I just keep saying the Lord's Prayer over and over. I don't get creative. I always seem to drift back into prayer. I'm not one to say okay, I'm going to pray now. It's just that I'm in that mode most of the time.

In terms of what I do for a living, I feel very strongly that all music and all singing is a prayer. I wrote "Family Bible" and I wrote "In God's Eyes" and both are prayers. Practically every song I write is a prayer in one way or another. I've always felt a spiritual element in any singing I've done, but in the past twenty years I've been more aware and thought about it more than I used to. I think it comes with living.

As for my advice on saying prayers, I will tell you, I had an ex-father-in-law who used to say, "Take my advice and do what you want to." That's what you need to do with prayer.

I recall Hank Williams saying he holds the pen and God does the writing and, being a songwriter, I have to agree with that. You work the controls and God flies the airplane.

Most recently, Laurence Fishburne has played Socrates Fortlow in HBO's *Always Outnumbered, Always Outgunned*. He also played Ike Turner in *What's Love Got to Do with It*, the boat gunner named Clean in the Francis Ford Coppola epic *Apocalypse Now*, and the father in *Boyz in the Hood*.

He related a very personal story that illustrates that prayer can indeed be a song.

What I have found is if I tune in to my heart and speak from my heart, then I'm on the right track. There are no set prayers. I mean, the only prayer that I was given was the Lord's Prayer. That's the only prayer I know by heart. But I have been about the business of speaking my truth and from my heart. And I would propose that if there were any words, that they would be "Thy will be done," and not mine.

There is no set time when I pray. Sometimes I pray silently and then there are times when I speak words aloud that are really powerful moments for me, but I don't think any more powerful than the silent prayers.

A time that stands out occurred when I was seventeen. I had worked in television since age ten, but, for whatever reason, I couldn't get a job anywhere. I was sitting on a bench somewhere in Hollywood and I was thinking about my situation and, I don't know why, but I started to sing a song.

I couldn't tell you the words, other than it

was about God, and it was like a chant of some kind. I improvised all the way through it and I recall just singing it over and over and over again. It was about the glory of God and the fact I was grateful to be a part of the divine spark. It made me feel a whole lot better. I got peace out of those moments and, I believe, a certain amount of power. I kept saying "Thank you." I wasn't asking for a job.

I DIDN'T think about it much when Pete Seeger first told me songs were prayers, but after Willie Nelson, David Crosby, and Laurence Fishburne all brought it up, I started to understand that a song was a pretty good foundation upon which to build a prayer. It got me thinking back to two particular instances years ago when I was doing my late-night radio show. I realized Pete Seeger wasn't the first to make this point to me. I simply hadn't been paying attention.

In December 1980, John Lennon was murdered outside the Dakota building in New York City. That evening I took calls from distraught Beatles fans about the loss they were feeling. I have always said the radio program was a mirror of America. That night the radio show reflected a country in shock. John Lennon's music touched millions. And more than one caller talked to me about his song "Imagine" and what a wonderful prayer it was.

And I remember July 18, 1981, when songwriter Harry Chapin was killed in an auto accident on the Long Island Expressway. Harry was probably best known for "Cat in the Cradle" and "Taxi," but he was also devoted to the cause of ending world hunger. That evening America's reflection in the mirror was again one of sadness. Harry Chapin fans called me to talk about where his words took them and how his songs, too, were prayers.

SO IT wasn't surprising when Kenny Rogers told us a powerful story about a moment of prayer that he shared with his audience the night his good friend Harry Chapin died. The concert was less than twelve hours after the accident.

When I go on stage it's much like anything else, it's like whatever you do for a living, you are on autopilot when you're there. But when Harry died . . . he was a friend of mine and he was the guy that started the whole world-hunger awareness, and that was the only time I had been a part of prayer on stage.

Harry had done something like a hundred and fifty concerts a year, with all the money going to hunger, and so that night I asked everyone, if they would, to help me for a moment and just say a silent prayer in their own way for Harry who had done so much for all of us. It's a little like the way we all felt when Princess Di died.

So we all took this moment of silence and I

could tell right away the audience was feeling this loss to the world as well. There was something special happening in the room. Everyone could feel it.

HARRY HAD a similar effect on his manager, Ken Kragen. After Harry's death, Kragen went on to organize and produce the hit singles "We Are the World" and "Hands Across America" which raised millions to fight hunger.

In 1985, about a week after we had recorded "We Are the World," I was in New York visiting various media and it was becoming very clear, very fast just how big this was going to be. The record wasn't out yet, but there was a lot of excitement.

I was in a car, being driven somewhere, and I got this distinct feeling Harry had crawled up inside me. I mean, I was doing it, but Harry was there orchestrating it. I'm scientific. I'm an astronomer. So this experience was, to say the least, unique. I had the sense Harry was in charge and what we were doing was under his guidance. I had said a prayer when he died and this was like he was answering. It was a profound moment in my life.

TODAY I know there are many songs which are prayers. Tunes like "My Prayer," "I Say a Little Prayer for You," "You'll Never Walk Alone," and so many more. As the rabbi often explained to me, answers are found right in front of you. My ears weren't open and, in some cases, my eyes haven't been either.

But now it is clear that Louis Armstrong's "What a Wonderful World," one of the many songs I can't sing — I can't sing anything, ask anyone who has heard me at dinner doing Bobby Darin tunes — but a song to which I've always felt a strong connection, is probably also a prayer.

And when you think about it, why would God or Allah or Buddha or whatever only want to hear from us via a set of rote words? Why not a song? Why not haiku? Why not a sonnet? Why not poetry? I was starting to understand, I thought. And it made me remember something else.

When I was growing up in Brooklyn, my parents were practicing Jews. I went along with it because I was a kid, but I never really embraced the meaning. Friday nights at our little apartment looked like a scene from *Fiddler on the Roof* with Shabbat candles, chicken soup, brisket, and overcooked vegetables. This tradition continued after my father died and I remember writing a prayer at age fourteen for my mother. It was a song.

> Good morning, Lord,
> How are you today?
> Good morning, Lord,

I'm going to pray.

You kept me through the night,
You shine a glowing light,
You teach me wrong from right
And send me on my way.

Sometimes I feel so happy,
Sometimes I'm sad.
But when you shine the sun
Nothing ever seems to be bad.

I pray someday to be with you,
Forever to say,
Good morning, Lord,
How are you today?

That was my song entitled "Good Morning, Lord" which was never published. However, I think it could have been a hit if Frankie Laine had gotten hold of it. It could have been the reverse side of "I Believe."

So seclude yourself in a quiet place, get as far as you can from distraction. (Relax any tension in your body; quiet all noise in your mind.) Then, envision yourself standing before God: there you are, mortal creature, beseeching the Infinite One. Pour out your heart, speak out your soul. Tell him what's on your mind. Without inhibitions, in whatever lan-

guage, say whatever comes to your mind.
— **RABBI KALONYMOUS
KALMAN SHAPIRA**

ACTOR ROD STEIGER, best known for his work in *On the Waterfront* and *In the Heat of the Night*, for which he won the Best Actor Academy Award in 1967, prays in a very individual, uninhibited way:

I call it conversations with whatever's out there. My favorite way of doing it is in the place of the beginning — the ocean or the water or the sea. When I really get down to having one of my serious conversations, I get in my pool, especially at night, with no clothes on, which is going back to the beginning, poetically speaking, the original womb: the ocean.

I have no set prayer. It can start with "I don't know what's going on. I really don't. Whoever is out there, I can't understand this." But I always thank whatever it is for protecting my home, saving the lives of my family from earthquakes, fires, floods, rains, and mudslides.

I take deep breaths and try to bring in the air from the ocean, and I will say, "Give me strength from the air that I breathe and the earth that I walk upon." I feel cleaner and I feel like I've at least spoken to somebody. It's the sharing of joy, but it can also be the shar-

ing of pain — those inner thoughts we all take around that can choke us to death sometimes. The water in the pool, the way I move slowly through it while I'm talking, lets me release all of this.

DELTA BURKE, formerly one of the stars of *Designing Women*, makes a connection between how she carries herself professionally and how she carries herself spiritually.

It's all a spiritual growth — a quest. When I would audition for shows, I'd go to forty auditions and not get anything. To keep myself going I would say, "Oh well, it wasn't meant to be and there's a reason it's not meant to be and there's something around the corner." The trouble is, after a while that corner seemed a long way away. I couldn't lose faith as an actress or I'd walk into an audition and just reek of failure.

You can't lose faith in the spiritual fashion either. It will become clear to you, but it doesn't always happen right away even though we wish it would.

Prayer has always had a cleansing feeling for me. In fact, one of my favorite places to pray is in the shower. It's a neat old tub-shower that I have, with steps leading up to it, and I put candles along the side and it is a peaceful place.

I don't go to church and I have no official

prayers. It's nothing more than talking to God from the heart.

KNOWN FOR his offbeat plots and inventive style, novelist Tom Robbins has entranced readers with his wry, irreverent humor in such modern classics as *Even Cowgirls Get the Blues*, *Skinny Legs and All*, *Still Life with Woodpecker*, and *Half Asleep in Frog Pajamas*. We had a chance to chat with Tom Robbins about his views on the subject of prayer.

Do you pray?

I pray every night, but not in the orthodox way. I'm not very adept at prayer because, being a writer, I'm overly cautious of my language. So, not wishing to bore whomever or whatever is on the receiving end with hackneyed phrases, and yet wondering at the same time whether ornamentation and witticism might be inappropriate or even unwelcome, I'm a little inhibited. Furthermore, I don't pray to any of the gods of organized religion because I'm not a religious person. I consider myself a spiritual person, and I draw a line of distinction between spirituality and religion — organized religion.

What religion were you brought up with?

Christian — Southern Baptist or Fundamental Protestantism. To me, religion is institutionalized spirituality. And the catch is spirituality doesn't lend itself to institutionalization.

It's my belief that the moment we attempt to organize religion, to organize spirituality, we destroy its essence. So religion then is spirituality and the spiritual has been killed. . . .

Do you believe God hears your prayers?

Yes. I prefer to say the Divine, because of all the anthropomorphic associations that we have with the word God. I don't object to the word God, I just don't want to limit it that way.

Do you feel God plays a role in your writing?

Yes, indirectly, but I never ask help of the Divine in my work. In fact, I try not to ask any kind of help from God in my prayers. I think a lot of prayer is nothing more than deity panhandling. People ask God for money, for cars, for girlfriends and boyfriends, and for help in their work. I don't think that's the Deity's function. At least, I don't know, I find something tacky about that. The only thing that I ask God for is protection and safety of my loved ones — and myself.

I think prayer is a website that the individual sets up in order to have a more direct relationship with the Godhead. And I think that the Deity, the Godhead, the universe, whatever you choose to call it — the mystery even, the Mystery with a capital M — is quite willing to connect with us if we give it an address. If we give it a code.

Spirituality, to me, refers to that state of being that a human individual occupies when he or she makes prolonged contact with the Mystery. It has to be personal and direct and one-on-one, and that's why, to me, prayer is maybe the highest form of worship.

What would you say was the most outstanding, meaningful, sensational prayer experience you've ever had?

Well, I have had what the Zen Buddhists call satori experiences, but they didn't come out of the process of prayer. . . . See, I think prayer can be shared with the whole being — with the body, not just with the voice.

Once when I was ill I was reading a book of movie criticism, and it made me want to see a film so badly that I got out of my sickbed — it wasn't anything serious, just the flu — and was driving into town to go to a movie. On my way, it began to snow very, very hard. It was a sudden blizzard and I could barely see a foot or two in front of the car; the snow was blowing right into the windshield. All around me were these white flakes. I was completely enveloped in them, as if in a void. And I passed a golf driving range — I couldn't see it, but it was there.

There was a sign advertising the driving range, and there was a golf ball on the sign, and the golf ball was outlined in white neon. So I looked up through all these energized flakes that were completely filling the atmosphere around me, and in the middle of this was this shining circle, also of white.

And for a few seconds I understood every-thing in the universe. I understood how every-thing is together. It was completely revealed to me. And, you know, I was transported. For days I felt a tingle up my spine. Of course, that revelation disappeared within a matter of seconds. . . .

So that wasn't prayer, but . . . I've been in that state a few other times, but it's always been something external and spontaneous, rather than being evoked by me calling on the Deity. And, yet, I connected very much to the Mystery. I don't think it's possible to be in that state without feeling this connection. I know it sounds a bit bizarre, but . . .

No, that's very powerful. Very powerful. Anything you'd like to add?

I try to offer thanks in prayers. My prayers are ninety percent expressions of gratitude, rather than asking for things.

Anything special you thank God for every day?

Well, being alive, first of all, and then my health, and the love in my life, and my literary talent, and the success that I've had — al-though that's probably way down the list.

Well, all the experts said "just do it" which left me a little cold, but after having inter-viewed a few artists, I was beginning to see that "just doing it" left itself wide open to some very individual interpretations.

COMEDY GREAT Alan King told us about the time he was cornered by his rabbi at a citizens' meeting. The rabbi wanted to know why Alan wasn't attending synagogue.

I told him, "Rabbi, I'm so busy." I did every cliché, but he just wouldn't let up. He had me. He was soft-spoken, but he kept coming at me. And finally I said, "Rabbi, do I have to present my credentials as a Jew?" I have a hospital here and so on and I listed all my credits. He kept saying, "Well, what does that have to do with not going to shul? You have time to watch television. You have time to read a book. You can come on Friday nights or come Saturday morning."

And I'm starting to get a little angry and so I said, "You know something, Rabbi? Every time I come to the synagogue and I walk in, and if I'm even a minute late, everybody says, 'There's Alan King. Look, there's Alan King.' I find that very disturbing." The rabbi said, "If you came more often, they wouldn't be that excited to see you!" I was wiped out.

Alan King still only attends shul about four times a year, but he told us about a moment in his life when he really needed a prayer.

I was standing on a street corner in Beverly Hills. I had a nine o'clock meeting at a restaurant and I was a little early. I'm just walking around looking in store windows and all of a sudden I hear these tires screeching.

I turned to look over my left shoulder and I

see a car out of control and the car is so close I can see it's an Oriental woman at the wheel. Like a bullfighter I moved to the side, and the car — it's maybe two feet away from me now — hits a traffic-light pole and stops. The car is totaled and the woman is taken to the hospital. A cop on a motorcycle sees the whole thing and later tells me, "Boy, Mr. King, that's as close as it's going to get."

So I went to the restaurant and had a cup of coffee and I'm shaking. I get up and leave. I got my car and went looking for a shul. I found a temple in Santa Monica and it was closed and I thought of the joke, if I was Catholic the church would be open.

Well, that night I'm supposed to meet people for dinner and I'm still shaken. I'm sitting in the restaurant and there was a young gentleman who recognized me and we start talking, and it turns out he's a rabbi. Well, I said I went looking for a shul this morning and couldn't find one open and I wanted to give thanks. It was instinctive.

The guy says "don't move" and he runs out to his car and brings back a book. He gave it to me and I still carry a page from that book with me all the time. Matter of fact, I've made copies of this prayer four or five times.

God in your universe who bestows good things on the guilty and who has bestowed every goodness upon me. May he who has bestowed goodness upon you continue to bestow every goodness upon you forever.

Rabbi Katsof later informed me that this is a traditional Jewish prayer.

ELLIOTT GOULD, well-known as the original Trapper John in the Robert Altman/Ring Lardner Jr. movie *M*A*S*H*, has made countless other movies of equal irreverence and humor. Elliott puts his heart into everything, and the metaphors were flying fast and furious when we discussed prayer.

I pray in my own way every day for peace and harmony, for my family and children, for humanity, nature, and the environment. When I feel I'm being swept away by materialism, by pressures, and by stress, I will pray just to get back in touch with my inner self.

I think prayer works for different people in different ways. I feel it's a vibration, a resonance, and a feeling that opens up channels into one's self that I believe are essential for circulation and for communication. Prayer helps to purify the soul, the heart, and the mind.

God, to me, is the mind — altogether. The universe is like a miraculous piece of music — every note, every molecule, every atom is part of a composition that wants to be played as well as it can be played. So, therefore, we must continue to practice. To live it. To live it with a conscience, a consciousness, an awareness of what we are in relation to that symphony.

Prayer is a sign of hope. It's an awareness that we are composed of perishable matter. Prayer puts oxygen in my cells. It reminds me that I'm still living and there's a chance for another moment — to detach from the outside and come back inside.

NOAH WYLE plays Dr. Ed Carter on the popular NBC series *ER*. He explained how prayer works for him, and cautioned up-front that it may not be the case for anyone else.

I'm actually between believing and praying to a higher power, and praying inwardly to myself. I vacillate between the power of positive thinking and the power of prayer and not quite knowing which is in existence at a particular time.

I do believe a lot of these issues are confidence issues and the energy that you feel toward yourself is what you reflect outward. And if you are praying to God and saying, "I'm insignificant, there's a bigger plan here, show me how I fit in," you're in essence checking back in with yourself and evaluating where this path so far has gotten you and where you want it to go from here.

STEVEN SEAGAL, star of popular action films such as *Under Siege*, *Executive Decision*, and *Marked for Death*, is also a Tibetan Buddhist and has been at the center of a controversy over his recognition as an incarnate Tibetan lama. Seagal says he was born with a serious spiritual sense and got his start in the late '60s visiting Zen monasteries in Japan and studying aikido and other martial arts.

He has always supported my efforts on behalf of the Larry King Cardiac Foundation with a donation of a signed movie poster or two for our popular silent auction. That's what he figured I was calling about, because his first words were, "What does the Cardiac Foundation need?" I told him I would certainly take a poster or two, but what I needed to talk with him about was prayer.

"Excuse me, Larry, for a moment I thought you said prayer."

"That's right," I told him. There was a pause. Seagal is a quiet man and when a quiet man is quiet, that's the most quiet of all.

Finally, he offered this guide for prayer from the perspective of a practicing Buddhist:

The key to the power of prayer is devotion. If you can have pure perception — which means you have no baggage of the self — you can realize people are as good as you make them. If you criticize those around you, then your path is inhibited. You are, in fact, looking for the good, the Buddha-nature in everyone.

91

You are taking away your own will, your own desire, your own grasp, and you are dissolving into this expanse that is a pure realm.

We are all born with the Buddha-nature in ourselves, the Christ-nature or whatever you believe your God is. But we're also born with natural obscurations that are a part of human nature that cause suffering. The society we live in, our social mores, also impart and teach us habitual tendencies that cause even more suffering. There are teachings that can be found in the Bible or the Buddha, however, that I liken to antidotes to the poisons that we have been born with and inherited in our lives.

And so I see it as a veil that we all have over us. And the more spiritual practice that we engage in, the thinner the veil becomes and eventually it is dissolved, and we see clear truth and light and love and compassion and kindness and the God within ourselves and others.

MANY OF us know Rene Russo from her starring roles in *Tin Cup*, *Get Shorty*, *Lethal Weapon*, *Outbreak*, and *Ransom*. At seventeen she began a modeling career that put her on the covers of national magazines and put money in her pocket. From the outside, Rene Russo had it all. However, from her inside perspective she was miserable. And thus began her self-described "very long road" in search of a spiritual life.

I talk to God like I'm talking to you. I pray in a simple way and I don't think there is a set way to do it. Something I hear over and over and over is people who feel like they're unworthy to pray and they don't know how to pray. Well, none of us knows all the answers and we're all struggling, so what I pray for is wisdom.

We all have a relationship with God and that should be respected no matter what religion we are. I'm just so firm on that. God will get us to where he wants us to be, so I pray for wisdom and discernment. Those are the big ones for me.

If there is something I'm worrying over or obsessing over, and I feel that it's just got me by the throat, I really try to just give it over to the Lord. I pray to have help with my fears and I pray for protection over my family and to be a good mother. I pray to strengthen my faith and to have the discipline to pray. And I also ask for discernment to know when I should keep my mouth shut.

There is a longstanding joke among people in radio about walking into an audition, seeing the usual faces sitting there waiting to be called to read for a commercial, and then Ken Nordine walks in. The minute he walks in the door everyone leaves, because Nordine is the best radio voice on the planet. If any other planets have radio, he's probably known there too.

The point here is that the people in the waiting room aren't praying that they get the part as much as they are praying Nordine won't show up. This case aside, though, prayer is common during auditions. I never asked Nordine about prayer because I never stayed around long enough to do it after he walked in.

We asked Rene Russo if she ever prayed to get an acting role.

There are certain things I have prayed for and I am so thankful I didn't get them. Here's what I do know: you can pray all you want, but the truth is God has more discernment than we do. I may think this is the best script that I've ever come across, although it is rare that has ever happened, but I will say, "Lord, if this is your will, I pray you give me favor." Everything is prefaced with this. "If it is your will, I pray you give me favor and help me with this script," or if I have to go on an interview, help with that so I do the best job possible.

That's what I pray for these days. It's let me do the best I can. I really see this as a partnership. I think if you just pray for the part you are missing the point. There's more to it. I want to feel I have done the best job I can do and then I honestly feel that's the point where it's out of my hands. If I don't get it, so be it. Maybe God wants to teach me humility.

WE ASKED Florence Henderson if there was ever a time when she prayed for an acting role and got it. And she told us this story:

When I was eighteen years old I had done the last national company tour of the musical Oklahoma *and there were plans to make it into a movie. I wanted to do a screen test for the movie and I prayed hard to get the job. I didn't get it and I remember thinking to myself how God didn't answer this prayer and what went wrong.*

Well, I had to go out and spend another year on the road with the stage production of Oklahoma *and in that year I learned more than I ever thought I could possibly learn about singing and acting. When the tour came to an end, I got a call to audition for the Broadway production of* Fanny *and I prayed really hard again to do well, and then after the audition I went back home to Indiana to wait for word from New York.*

I went to this little monastery in my hometown and Father Gerard had a little service for me and we prayed I would get the role. I remember saying if I get the job I'll give my first check to the monastery. I went home and that very same day a telegram arrived from Josh Logan, the great director, saying, "Come back to New York, Fanny. We await your arrival."

I was in the show for two years and it turned out to be the greatest answer to a prayer that anyone could have had, even if it wasn't what I had originally sought.

As a postscript, Florence Henderson did send her first paycheck to the monastery, but was quick to add that it wasn't bargaining. She saw the check as payment for a special service performed at her request and never doubted her prayer. "I was confident," she said.

I asked God for all things I might enjoy in life and, instead, God gave me life so that I may enjoy all things.
— ANONYMOUS

LOU DIAMOND PHILLIPS, who portrayed singer Ritchie Valens in the film *La Bamba* and King Mongkut, the King of Siam, in the stage production of *The King and I*, told us he doesn't pray to get the part.

There are times when I have prayed before an audition and I have always prayed that it would just work out, but I always annex the prayer with the words "Help me to accept what is."

I'm not one of those people who believes that you pray for rain one day and if it doesn't pour from the sky that God has let you down. I don't think it works that way. At an audition I'm praying for an open heart and an open mind and the confidence to go in and do my best and to present myself in all of my ability. And also to keep from shooting myself in the foot by letting negative energy get the best of me with fear or nervousness or pride.

Prayer at this time is a reminder of who I am, how I got to where I am, and that I am blessed with some talent. Many times, I pray to God to, as Samson did, return my strength to its full power.

Can you tell me a little about your role in *The King and I* as it relates to prayer and spirituality?

King Mongkut was a monk for about seven years prior to becoming king. He was on a very spiritual path and he was trying to re-think Buddhism. There were a lot of different influences — superstitions, folklore, influences from Burma and Asia — that had influenced the beliefs of his own people. He went back to the basics and reapplied the original thinking of his forefathers and brought back a much simpler and much more pure form of religion.

As I was doing my research for the role, there were certain aspects of the real man that I wanted to inject into the character to make him whole and less of a caricature, and one of those things was spirituality. I would find places within the show to pray. One of the most difficult times was at the end — on his deathbed. There was a good five-minute period where I would sit on stage in full view of the audience as another scene took place. That gave me a chance, every single day, to say, "This is my time to pray."

Did you ever get so involved in prayer that you forgot your cue?

Fortunately, no. There were times when I was so involved in prayer I would hear my cue and know in my mind that I wasn't finished. I would have to say, "I'm sorry, God, but I have to hurry up and speak a little faster now. I'll get back to you later."

Every day I would take stock of the show, the people in it, and the audience because I was very, very grateful for it. Every single day we were touching the lives of twelve hundred to fourteen hundred people. My prayer was, "I hope their lives are richer and happier when they leave the theatre." In essence, the theatre became a temple.

AND THEN there is Goldie Hawn — producer, director, Academy Award-winning actress. She is loved the world over as a source of laughter and joy in countless film roles, yet she considers her most important role is that of mother to her three children. She believes that as we approach the millennium we are soon to encounter a time of intense spiritual awareness and was glad to offer her thoughts on prayer, as it is a daily activity for her.

I've been praying since I was a little girl. I'd have my own private moments talking to God, and I found such peace. My mother told me, "You don't have to go to a church or a syna-

gogue to pray." I remembered that — that I could talk to God wherever I was.

So I'd sit in my room sometimes and I was frightened of the dark, frightened of the unknown, frightened of death and things I didn't understand. And the Twenty-third Psalm — I used to read the Bible by myself — this psalm brought such peace to me. It was the part that says, "Yea, though I walk through the valley of the shadow of death, I will fear no evil: for thou art with me; thy rod and thy staff they comfort me."

This meant so much to me, because for me this rod was a symbol of the deep connection between me and the light and the power and the glory of God, of the beauty and the positive energies I could feel. It brought me such peace that I would fall off to sleep.

What kinds of things do you pray for now?

I always start with health because it's the most important thing. Money is the least of my prayers. It doesn't really enter into my prayers. I also pray to receive the light of God, the energy — the positive energy — because I know that I'm an instrument.

I feel that if I empty my ego, empty all these things that I identify with being me, the I — oh, you know, how we see the image of ourselves — and let that go, then I can receive God's energy and then I can give back.

One of my biggest prayers is to be an instrument of God's light and give back to my family and the people I come in contact with, and on a higher level, because I've been given this life, this time, this place where I can do some good. I'm so thankful and humbled by that.

Do you feel your prayers are answered or heard?

I don't know if it's someone hearing my prayers. I used to think God had a long beard and I could see him in man's form. But as I've gotten older, I think that there's a supreme consciousness. I think there is an order. I think we are all made by the light. We come from light and we go to light, and I believe that light is supreme. When I imagine God, I imagine this incredible light that is perfection.

If we let go and allow ourselves to understand that we were created by God, by this entity of energy in perfect form, we understand that we are perfect. We're as perfect as the leaf. We're as perfect as the universe. Everything has its place.

A part comes and goes, a piece of jewelry comes and goes, money comes and goes, but you can't be happy with things unless your soul is filled with light. My goal is to feel joy in my heart.

RABBI KATSOF and I hadn't talked in a while, so I called to update him.

"Well, Irwin, artists certainly aren't experts,

but they do speak from the heart."

"Right. Connection to God starts with the mind. You use your intelligence to understand God, but then you must make it real, you must move it into your heart. But there's another step. The next step is to express it in your actions throughout the day."

"Rabbi, this is getting too complicated."

"Well, life is complicated. Life is heavy."

"It shouldn't be so difficult."

"Live television is difficult, but you do it every day with no rehearsal — one chance."

"But that's television. I just do it."

"You said it, not me."

We hung up and as was becoming the case after a phone conversation with the rabbi, I quietly thought about the topic. I had the feeling I was finally connecting to the subject — not to God because, well, you know I'm looking for proof — but that my heart and mind were coming together.

I looked out the big picture window overlooking the Washington, D.C., skyline and saw the sun glistening on the Potomac River. The cherry blossoms were blooming and spring was in the air. I sensed there was some kind of a natural movement going on. That's when I started belting out those wonderful words about a wonderful world that I first heard sung by Satchmo so many years ago.

Chapter Four
Prayer and Our Leaders

During a speaking engagement in Los Angeles, I shared the podium with former British Prime Minister Margaret Thatcher.

After we delivered our talks, I spent a few moments with her at a reception after the event. We spoke about the new prime minister, Tony Blair, and the challenges he faced. We covered a variety of foreign affairs issues, and then I asked her about prayer. I was asking a lot of people about prayer.

Thatcher looked me right in the eye and said, "I do pray, but I don't like to talk about it because I've always regarded prayer as the most personal of matters."

The next morning when the rabbi called to check in, I put a question to him. "Do the prayers of leaders bear more weight than the prayers of someone like me?"

"You're praying, Larry. Congratulations."

"I'm just using myself as an example of someone ordinary."

"You're ordinary?"

"Irwin, please, I'm asking a question here. Doesn't it make sense that the needs of a leader, a president or a prime minister, should take precedence because that person makes decisions every day that will affect millions of lives? I mean, out of all the people on earth, the leaders, whatever their title, ought to have a hotline to God. Their prayers should get priority so they can get some divine guidance for decisions that affect the world, decisions about war and economics, or poverty and hunger."

Silence. "Hello? Irwin?" What a shame it would be to lose another of my cogent perspectives on prayer in one of the rabbi's silences. Then it dawned on me. "You're praying again, aren't you?"

"Larry, you're a quick study, no matter what others might say. It's an interesting question, but to my understanding, God hears everyone's prayers. God doesn't hear one voice over another, be it a president or a pauper, you or me."

"I can't believe that, Irwin. The prayers of a president or a prime minister have to be more important, they need to be heard."

"Larry, God doesn't work in the same time and space continuum that you and I do. We can only do so many things at once before we get overloaded, but God is beyond that."

"I don't care what continuum he's in. God has to pay more attention to the prayers of leaders."

"I'll tell you what," the rabbi said, "let me get my teacher, Rabbi Noah Weinberg, on conference call to talk about this because it's a good question. So let's figure it out."

"Okay. When? I'm just going out for my walk," I said.

"Take your cell phone. I'll call as soon as I get him."

I usually go to a high school track near the hotel for my morning walk, and figured it would take the rabbi some time to set up this call, but no sooner had I laced up my sneakers than the phone rang.

"Larry, I have Rabbi Weinberg on the phone from Israel."

"What took you so long?"

"Irwin tells me you have a question," Rabbi Weinberg said, "but first, how are you?"

"I'm fine, Rabbi. And you?"

"Good, thank God. So what's your question?"

"I asked whether God listens to the prayers of leaders more than those of ordinary people, and Irwin says no. I think that's ridiculous."

"God does listen to the prayers of leaders more, but they must be righteous leaders with pure intentions whose concerns are for all humanity. God will not listen to a Hitler or a Stalin."

"So I was right."

"You were right. Irwin, you must be doing a very good job. The student is now teaching the teacher. Have you told him about the thirty-six?"

"The thirty-six what?" I wondered.

"Tell him about the thirty-six, Irwin."

With that, Rabbi Weinberg wished us good luck on the book and said goodbye. I am always amazed at how calm and peaceful certain religious people are. I first met Rabbi Weinberg at one of the fund-raisers. Like the Dalai Lama, he never seems to lose his balance, not even when trying to explain a simple idea to a dunce like me.

"So what's the thirty-six, Irwin?"

"It's a Jewish folk tale, a myth that every generation has thirty-six righteous people. Their faith and belief in God sustains the world. It is through their merit and their worthiness that the world is held in balance."

"Now that would be somebody to talk to about prayer. I don't suppose you've met any, have you?"

"Nobody knows who they are. They're usually thought to be very simple people who perform good deeds all their lives and their goodness goes out into the rest of us which, if we pay attention, will make us better. It's their deeds and their actions that are important. They are not caught up in the pettiness of life. Instead, their desire is to help humanity."

"Irwin, I gotta tell you something."

"What's that?"

"I'm not one of the thirty-six."

"Thanks for the news flash, Larry."

Forty-eight percent of Americans pray for the president of the United States.
— GALLUP POLL (1993)

ON THE night before Gerald Ford was to be sworn in as the thirty-seventh president of the United States, replacing Richard Nixon who resigned the office in the wake of the Watergate scandal, he and his family gathered in their Alexandria, Virginia, home. It was August 8, 1974.

All that day my wife and I were at our home and we prayed jointly for guidance. Following the swearing-in the next day, I think that prayer was very helpful in giving me both guidance and assurance for the responsibilities I was about to assume as president.

The next evening, President Ford addressed the nation and his introduction to America included these words:

"I am acutely aware that you have not elected me as your president by your ballots. So I ask you to confirm me with your prayers."

Prayer is an integral part of President Ford's life — before, during, and after his days in the White House.

I definitely pray, and have most of my life. I do it because of a tradition in our family and because, at my current age, it means a great deal to me on a personal basis. I pray every

106

night when I go to bed. It's a daily routine. I start with a prayer that is very meaningful to me and has been for many, many years: "Trust in the Lord with all thine heart; and lean not unto thine own understanding. In all thy ways acknowledge him and he shall direct thy paths." I pray for my family. I pray for close friends who have health problems or other challenges.

What do you get out of prayer?

That's very subjective. It's always had a great impact on making me feel good about the future.

How do you envision God?

I look upon him as a higher power, somebody who has a role bigger than any one of us, a role that encompasses the world. As my higher power, I look upon God as one who gives me guidance and help.

FORMER PRESIDENT JIMMY CARTER came to the White House saying he would continue to be as involved in prayer there as he was at the Governor's Mansion in Atlanta, Georgia. He had come to Atlanta saying he would be as involved in prayer there as he was in Plains, Georgia, where he taught Sunday school.

Did your routine for prayer change when you became president?

I would say my routine of reading the Bible each night with Rosalynn and praying at the

First Baptist Church in Washington or, more often, at a special service at Camp David, was the same pattern I had in Plains and when I was governor of Georgia, but I prayed more often and fervently as president. I had a tremendous responsibility.

I wanted to benefit from God's help, to have the maturity and sound judgment to make the right decisions. I had a little private room next to the Oval Office, and when I was in a quandary I would go there and pray I would make the right decision. It was a place to pray, but I never prayed for favors, like for Navy to beat Army.

You didn't pray for the Braves last night? (Atlanta had lost the National League Pennant to the Florida Marlins.)

Maybe I should have.

Tell me about the days leading up to and during the Camp David Peace Summit with Israeli Prime Minister Menachem Begin and Egyptian President Anwar Sadat.

When we went to Camp David on September 5, 1978, Begin, Sadat, and I all wanted to pray. But before our first talks, I spent several hours negotiating the text of the prayer. I got a proposed draft from a prayer group in Washington and I made some edits. Sadat approved it, Begin made some changes, and we issued the prayer the first day.

Conscious of the grave issues that face

us, we place our trust in the God of our fathers from whom we seek wisdom and guidance. As we meet here at Camp David, we ask people of all faiths to pray with us that peace and justice may result from our deliberations.

All of us were religious and Sadat talked about his religion all the time. He would say we all worshiped the same God, which made Begin uncomfortable. While we were at Camp David those thirteen days, Begin and Sadat were almost totally incompatible. They didn't like each other and kept resurrecting ancient grievances. So after the third day I wouldn't let them see each other again.

There are stories the talks almost ended without a resolution a number of times.

I remember one day, maybe the tenth, Sadat told Moshe Dayan he would make no more concessions in the negotiating text that I was carrying back and forth. Sadat told his people at Camp David to pack, and he told National Security Adviser Zbigniew Brzezinski to arrange a helicopter to take them back to Washington.

I was in my cabin talking to Secretary of Defense Harold Brown and others about budget matters. I was in jeans and a T-shirt. I remember changing into a suit and going to Sadat's cabin, where I had a very sharp exchange with him. I accused him of breaking promises he had made. Then I went outside to a quiet place by myself and prayed.

The Camp David peace accords were signed three days later, on September 17, in a ceremony at the White House. During the Camp David Summit, Jimmy Carter also had to tend to the business of being president. On September 11, the seven-day point in the Camp David dialogue, President Carter had a conversation reassuring the Shah of Iran that the United States could be counted on for assistance and support.

A week later, *Time* magazine ran a cover story titled "Iran in Turmoil." It would prove to be prophetic, as the Shah was forced into exile when the Ayatollah Khomeini and the Muslim clerics assumed power in Iran. The following year, sixty-six Americans were taken hostage when fundamentalist revolutionary forces stormed the U.S. Embassy in Tehran.

The moment you found out what happened in Iran — how soon after did you pray?

I remember precisely when I prayed. It was immediate. Whenever a crisis occurs, it has always been my habit to say a prayer. 1980 was a year when prayer was a very important part of my life. It was a crisis year. We were faced with the Soviet invasion of Afghanistan and the hostages had been taken and I was trying to preserve peace.

Did you ask God in these prayers, "Why are you doing this?"

First of all, God always answers prayers. Sometimes it's "yes" and sometimes the answer is "no," and sometimes it's "you gotta be kidding." But when prayers are not answered the way we want them, then we have an opportunity and an obligation to reexamine our own position. Maybe the things for which we are praying aren't God's will. I don't question God about whether or not he has taken care of my needs. Prayer is an association and a conversation for enlightenment and guidance.

Did you ever pray for the Ayatollah?

I asked for God's guidance or Allah's guidance or for the Supreme Being to induce the Ayatollah to live within the parameters of the Koran. I was praying he would treat the hostages humanely. I would say, in retrospect, all those prayers were answered. The hostages were released, they were safe, they all came home.

Why do you think God made you, and the hostages, wait 444 days?

I don't think God works with our time schedules and specific goals. It isn't proper to expect God to do that and I certainly never asked him to do that.

Is there a right way to pray?

Prayer is how we communicate with God. One of the advantages of the Christian faith is that we see God represented as a human being. It's a personal relationship, so each will be different. I always begin every prayer with the words "In the name of Christ."

Do you think God hears the prayers of a president more than those of the people the president governs?

No.

In my opinion, President Carter is the best former president this nation has ever had. He has continued to work for peace, freedom, and democracy through his nonprofit Carter Center in Atlanta and he builds homes with the poor as a volunteer for Habitat for Humanity. I was thinking about telling the president about the thirty-six, but decided if anyone would know about that, it would be him.

BARBARA BUSH told me about her prayers before, during, and after her days at the White House.

George and I pray every night together, by phone if we are in different cities. We have been doing this ever since we've been married. We never pray for financial gain or political victory — we have prayed for health of family and friends. We prayed during the Gulf War for the safety of everybody's return. That was constantly on our minds.

We both believe our prayers have been answered, but then we have never prayed for the miraculous — like terminal illness being cured tomorrow. I can say I feel relieved after having said prayers.

SHIMON PERES was Israel's prime minister from 1984 to 1986, and in 1995 he assumed the role of acting prime minister of Israel following the assassination of Yitzhak Rabin and then lost in a direct election to Benjamin Netanyahu in May of 1996.

Shimon Peres's military/political career began back in 1947 when he was responsible for arms purchases during Israel's War of Independence. A year later he was promoted to head of Naval Services. He was minister of defense from 1974 to 1977, and was instrumental in planning the bold raid on the Entebbe airport to rescue more than one hundred hostages from an Air France jet that was hijacked by Palestinian terrorists.

He won the Nobel Peace Prize in 1994, along with Yitzhak Rabin and Yassir Arafat, for the historic peace treaty he signed with the PLO that paved the way for Palestinian self-rule in Israeli-occupied territory.

Do you have a set routine for prayer?

I pray at the Wailing Wall when the occasion calls for it. I pray at different occasions like a marriage, a bar mitzvah, or a death. Or when I have a piece of bread on Saturday or a glass of wine. It's not constant, but I pray from time to time.

Do you have a particular prayer that you say?

I usually ad-lib my prayers. I always pray for peace or in memory of somebody.

Why peace?

Because the failure to find peace has killed more people than any other human failure. We have to depart from this sickness that is spread throughout human annals because we are entering an epoch where we don't need wars. Our own country has gone through five wars and so many young people have been killed — so many families are so tragically alone and in deep sorrow.

When you had to make a decision to send your soldiers into action, did you pray before making that decision?

On many occasions I did, in my heart. Before making the decision, I would think very carefully how to avoid the killing of people. I prayed there would not be bloodshed and that our soldiers would come back home — the greatest victory is when the soldier comes back home.

It wasn't glory that guided me, but real life. I have a deep respect for life. That's what makes me a human being. And if you don't respect the life not only of yourself but of others, you are not really a human being in my judgment.

Do you pray for both sides to come back?

Mostly for our own side, but it is a hidden tradition in Israel that one respects the lives of others. On many occasions we made a su-

preme effort not to take the life of our enemies. In our way, we see every war fought twice — once in the battlefields and then in the history books. You don't want to win in one and lose in the other. So here, too, you are very careful.

How do you think prayer works?

It is committing yourself to something which is above you, be it the Lord or your conscience, but it's a special effort to be as close as possible to something that is nobler and higher. . . .

Can anybody do this or does it require preparation?

I have to prepare myself, but some prayers are the matter of a group of people. When the Jewish people are praying on Yom Kippur, it is a personal time but also a public coming together. Once, when my grandfather was leading the prayers of Yom Kippur, I was deeply moved. When I think of this day, I am returned to the history of my people. Now, when I hear the prayers on Yom Kippur, I am moved deep to my bones.

I remember the words and I remember the tunes and I feel all of a sudden elated and that I can fly into a higher atmosphere.

Do you think you and Yassir Arafat pray to the same God?

I think, yes. And not only the same God, but he claims the same father, Abraham. I remember telling King Hussein if all of us are sons of Abraham, why didn't we become brothers?

Do you pray for Yassir Arafat?

I don't pray for Yassir Arafat, but I consider his needs and I respect his side of the story. I understand perfectly well that my praying will not turn Yassir Arafat into a Zionist. Even if it's the same Lord, it's not the same people. Even if it's the same situation, it's not the same history.

I respect very much what he stands for and pray for the success of his people, because I feel very strongly that the more successful the Palestinians become, the more successful peace we shall achieve.

Do you talk to God about how long this process of peace seems to take?

No. I recall the Jewish philosopher Franz Rosenzweig who said that the Lord is responsible only for the nice part of history. He wouldn't take responsibility for the evil parts. And then I agree with the French author Flaubert who said there is a division between men and God. He in heaven is responsible for the beginning and for the end. We on earth are responsible for the in-between.

Tell me some experiences you've had with unanswered prayers.

On all those occasions when death came, I felt prayers wouldn't help. I went through many terrible experiences. I would go to the square in Jerusalem after a bomb had ex-

ploded and the whole square was filled with blood and the eyes of the people were filled with tears and many were calling me a traitor or a killer. I felt they had nobody to turn on.

Whenever I go to a Holocaust memorial, or when I go to the cemetery and see the young people lying there, I feel that all our prayers failed. So I know that not all prayers will be answered. Yet, in spite of this revolting feeling, I remain a great believer. I think our whole life would be extremely tough without believing and without praying.

I know the Jewish people could never exist without prayers. What keeps us together is not our land and not our army for the last two thousand years. What keeps us together is prayer.

We are asking people to contribute a prayer for this book. Do you have a contribution?

I would offer the one sentence Moses told the people and is the basis of Judaism: "Love thy neighbor as thyself."

How should one go about prayer?

The most important thing to understand is that prayer must be very sincere and come from within. The worst thing is to look upon prayer as a sermon, a ceremony, a cult. In my judgment, this is a corruption of prayer.

The promise of prayer is that you do it straight to heaven and straight to the Lord without any intermediaries and without any public relations. This is straight from your heart, from the depth of your being, and from the meaning of your existence.

When Yitzhak Rabin died, did you pray?

We know now the murderer didn't know who to kill first — Yitzhak or me. We were apart by maybe fifteen feet. I didn't know that he was fatally shot. I went to the hospital and Yitzhak was struggling between life and death. The head of the hospital told me there was a slight chance, but ten minutes later he returned and told me he was dead.

So I went to the place where he lay, the bed. I kissed him on the forehead and I told him farewell. . . . This was between him and me, without witnesses. And I started thinking — and this may be symbolic — a few minutes earlier we were standing together with the singers and we were singing, "Let peace come. Let the morning arrive."

Neither of us were famous singers so we were given a piece of paper with the words of the song. And then he folded the paper and put it in the pocket of his jacket. A few minutes later this song was penetrated together with his heart. I thought that was something very moving.

Why do you think that happened?

Many will try to explain it. I believe you don't have to explain everything. Many of the things that happen in life, symbolic or otherwise, let them remain as they are — a question without an answer.

I was nibbling an onion bagel with coffee on the sidewalk outside the Carnegie Deli in New York City while the rabbi sipped his Diet Snapple.

As we stood at the corner of Seventh Avenue and Fifty-fifth Street, Rabbi Katsof asked if I knew the definition of a foxhole prayer, as in the expression "When the bullets are flying there's no such thing as an atheist in a foxhole."

In between bites I said, "A foxhole prayer is when you think you're going to die or when you're at the end of your rope and you think things can't get any worse, so you figure what do I have to lose?"

Irwin silently studied me.

"That's all I know, it's the most horrible event in your life and you start praying because . . ." I couldn't finish the sentence. "Help me out here, Rabbi."

"That's exactly right. You said it. Help me out. Life can be complicated and demanding whether you are president of the United States

119

or a television talk show host. Sometimes we don't have time to think about God. So from time to time God will try to get our attention. If we miss the first hint, then God will nudge us a little harder until we pay attention. When bad things happen, we usually start to pay attention. It's God's way of reminding us to include him in our lives. When you think about it, that's not a big request at all."

"Let me understand this," I said, "you're saying bad things happen because we haven't paid attention to God?"

"No, bad things happen because we live in life. But, for whatever reason, many of us only pay attention to God when bad things happen. Here's a short story. . . ."

More short stories? I was just going to say something, but I realized that I actually liked most of his stories and I seemed to be learning something from them.

"An uncle has a nephew in college who never writes. So the uncle sends a brief note asking the nephew about his classes, his major, and so on. Then he ends the note saying he has enclosed a check for one hundred dollars because college can have unexpected costs. But the uncle doesn't include the check.

"Boom! Within four days there's a letter from the nephew saying things are fine, classes are interesting, how are you, let's get together for your birthday, blah, blah, blah, and then adds a line saying 'By the way, you forgot to enclose the check.' God does the same thing. He sends us moments that will get our attention and re-focus us. But if you aren't listening, then how can you expect to hear, and if you aren't look-ing, how can you expect to see?"

"You gotta admit, Irwin, it would make the whole thing easier if he'd just have a couple of one-on-ones with us from time to time. Y'know, 'This needs improvement and this ain't too good, but this turned out okay,' and like that."

At that moment, a young child stepped off the curb on Seventh Avenue into the oncoming traffic. Her mother, who was buying a *New York Post* at a newsstand, leaped into the street, grabbed the child, and pulled her back onto the sidewalk. The mother was visibly shaken as she stooped down, shook her daughter by the shoulders, and scolded her before whacking her once on the backside. The child was in tears as they walked away.

Rabbi Katsof turned to me. "Right here in front of you is an example of what we're talking about. That mother got her daughter's atten-tion. She did it because she loves the child. Par-ents must get their children to focus just as God gets his children to focus. Times of crisis are God's message to us to start paying atten-tion." For a moment the rabbi was quiet as he searched the crowded street for the mother and daughter, but they had disappeared. "I was just wondering," he said, "if this experience was a message from God so that you will understand."

"Why should a child have to be spanked to teach me a lesson?"

"God didn't spank the child to teach you. That was the child's lesson, but the fact you were there to see it was your message. From our limited perspective, we may say the mother was cruel, just as we sometimes think God is cruel. God sees the larger perspective, he sees the big picture, he knows what you really need."

"So, what was the message?"

"One of the ways God talks to us is through pain. Where's your pain? Where are you hurting? Look deep inside. That's God's kindness, he's letting you know you're headed in the wrong direction. Where are you going, Larry?"

"In general, I'm not sure. But right now, I better get back to work."

The rabbi said his goodbyes and then disappeared into the crowd much the same way a mother and her child had done just moments earlier.

I hated to admit it, even to myself, but a lot of what he said was starting to make sense.

We turn to God for help when our foundations are shaking only to learn that it is God shaking them.
— CHARLES WEST
THEOLOGIAN,
PRINCETON THEOLOGICAL SEMINARY

THE GOOD thing about the current media explosion is that I could watch sports all day on ESPN. The bad thing is that it has spawned too many tabloid television programs.

Gossip has become news, and we have all become somewhat like onlookers at a bad traffic accident — you don't want to look but you do. We've created an industry based on other people's misfortunes and, unfortunately, the more fortune or celebrity you have then all the better for the story.

Actress Mia Farrow knows this all too well. She was staked out and stalked by paparazzi, as well as by the so-called legitimate media, in the wake of the sensational story of her breakup with Woody Allen.

I grew up in a devoutly Catholic family. We said our prayers when we woke up and as soon as we got to school, where there was also an hour each day of religion class. We said grace before each meal and the rosary, or a good chunk of it, each night in front of a large, beautifully carved crucifix that had belonged to my grandfather. As a child I prayed spontaneously, and particularly intensely in times of trouble. God was very real to me.

Did you blame God during those troubled times?

I did say, and more than once, "Where were you? Who was on watch, and how could you let this happen?" I was focused on the damage to my children who had been pro-

foundly hurt, shocked, and bewildered. I needed to talk to them but I didn't know what to say. Nothing made sense. I remember praying for guidance on how to help my children through that terrible time without being diminished by it.

Finally, I gathered the older kids together in the kitchen and told them, "We have seen firsthand that there are terrible consequences to terrible acts and, therefore, how crucial it is that we proceed through our lives with respect for others and be guided by a sense of responsibility."

So much was lost — people I loved dearly and my belief in them, daily life as we knew it, our privacy and peace. We did not bring these troubles upon ourselves, but through them I was determined to define myself to others, and to God.

Each laceration became a test, a trial. Each scalding survived was a purification. Each plunge into darkness left me struggling for light. Every separate fear and personal humiliation endured served to strip away what was nonessential in me and made me understand: it is by that which cannot be taken away that we can define ourselves.

I still pray in a pinch, but I try not to restrict it to that. The ideal that I strive for is to make my entire day a prayer, to make my life a prayer. This sounds far too grandiose an aspiration — I mean, I'm an actress not a nun — but I can try.

One of my sons came up with a metaphor that I like a lot. He had disappointed himself on some occasion and he came to me in tears and said, "It's so difficult being a human being. It's like a garden you have to weed every day." That is so accurate. So, in my times of silence, reflection, and prayer, I try to weed out those things that are undesirable, unworthy, and unnecessary — to keep things as simple and as pure as possible.

SUZANNE SOMERS told me that prayers for her child transformed her life. She made a bargain with God: If he would save her son, she would dedicate her life to being the best person she could be. Bargaining is a controversial element in prayer. Gallup conducted a poll in December of 1993 that discovered sixty-eight percent of Americans said they do not make bargains in prayer and thirty-one percent said that they did.

Somers was brought up Catholic. She was enrolled in a Catholic girls' college, but at age seventeen she became pregnant and was asked to leave. She married the baby's father and they divorced a year and a half later. Because of that, the Catholic Church told her she could no longer be a part of its membership. And at age eighteen, she began what she calls "an inner dialogue" which continues to this day.

Her foxhole prayer came one horrible day

when her three-year-old son was involved in an accident.

He was run over by a car, missing his head but crushing his spleen. Everything seemed to be happening in a blur as if it was all under water. The ambulance took him to the emergency room, and I remember hearing a doctor say, "He has a fifty-fifty chance to live." My child was taken into surgery and I sat there thinking to myself, "This can't really be happening." After what seemed like an interminable amount of time, the doctors came out of surgery and told me I should go home and change my clothes, which were still covered with blood. So I did just that.

And then, for reasons that I still don't understand, I started cleaning. I cleaned his room. I organized his toys. I scrubbed floors. All the time I was doing that, I was saying, "If you let him live, I promise I will spend the rest of my life being the best person I can be." That was a bargain I've tried to keep because he did live.

The road back for both mother and son wasn't easy. That horrible day was the beginning of the road to recovery, not only for her son but for Suzanne as well.

When he returned from the hospital he would wake up screaming from horrible nightmares. I'd hold him, praying for help, but his dreams got worse. Finally, I took him to a community mental health center where we both spent a year in therapy and flourished.

Our therapist then decided my son would be fine, but wanted me to continue seeing a counselor since she knew about my having grown up in an alcoholic family and the accompanying low self-esteem. I was in treatment for three years. Now I look at my childhood, that accident, and therapy as somebody shaking my shoulders saying, "Wake up! Pay attention! Look at what's important and seek where you can add to the world rather than take away."

ALAN DERSHOWITZ is a noted defense attorney, prolific writer, and teacher at Harvard Law School. Alan had a conversation with Rabbi Katsof about his bargain with God for his son's health.

Any special prayer that you really remember that you feel God answered — something very powerful?

My son Elan was very sick when he was ten years old. He had a brain tumor. And the doctors, or at least some of the doctors, thought it was hopeless. I did a lot of praying, I did a lot of arguing. I was alternately angry and frightened, and prayerful. One doctor was very pessimistic and another doctor was cautiously encouraging.

I mean, it was not something that everybody said was hopeless, but it was not an en-

couraging prognosis when we got it. It was the single most frightening event of my life because, you know, lawyers need to be in control. And when we're out of control, when it's beyond our control, we feel frustrated.

So your son got better?

My son got better and he's had a wonderful — thank God — a wonderful, wonderful life. And so he's fine.

Did you say anything to God afterwards?

In my own way. I mean, I made certain commitments and promises. I've never talked about this to anybody. This happened in the early '70s, and I devoted virtually all of the '70s to representing Jews in trouble for free.

Because of the prayers for your son getting better?

Yes. I mean, that was my commitment, that was my deal. I spent the '70s representing Russian Jews. I represented kids from the Jewish Defense League who were in trouble. And it's interesting, because during the Russian and Jewish Defense League cases, I felt that I helped save a couple of lives. And for me it was very important at that point to pay back and save a life.

I represented the people who had hijacked the airplane from Leningrad, who were facing the death penalty. Sharansky came a little later in the '70s, but in '73, right after Elan's surgery, I took on the case involving the

Jewish Defense League. These kids were facing a possible death penalty for planting a bomb in Sol Hurok's office.

I must have had seven or eight death penalty cases during the '70s. And every time I won — we won them all, we won all seven of the cases — I felt it was a little bit of a paying back for the dead. I couldn't save lives through surgery, I didn't know how to do that, so I was able to save some lives through law. There's no question, from my perspective, that the '70s was a decade of paying back on some promises I had made to myself and to God.

Has anything like that happened since the '70s that was as powerful for you?

One hopes one goes through a situation like that only once in a lifetime. I don't wish it on anybody else, even though both for my son and for me it was a building experience. In the end, it was an experience that I think helped us both live better lives. It's not something I would wish on anybody, obviously — to go through a near-death experience with a son. There's nothing quite like it. That is the formative experience of my adult life, my son's illness. It changed me in every possible way.

Do you believe that there is a personal God that answers your prayers?

What I find very hard to accept is a God that needs to be praised. I think if there is a God, he's sitting up there saying, "Stop praising me already. You're praising me for your own good, not for my good. I don't need to be praised so much. A good person doesn't need to be praised so much, so a good God doesn't need to be praised all the time." I wonder about that. I think there are prayers that human beings have created in a sense of awe and frustration.

But I can't believe that God would want us constantly to treat him like a king. I also don't believe God will punish you if you question him. I don't want to make analogies between myself and God, but my favorite students are the ones that question everything I say, all the time. So my God is a God who is prepared to engage in a dialogue and not just one-way praise.

No man ever prayed heartily without learning something.
— RALPH WALDO EMERSON,
"NATURE" (ESSAY)

RABBI KATSOF and I were at my apartment in Arlington, Virginia, having coffee and Diet Snapple as we talked about — what else? — prayer.

"We learn from the hard stuff, not the easy stuff," the rabbi told me. "Prayer is a natural need, even for agnostics."

That got my attention. "What do you mean?"

"Think of the worst moment in your life, a time when you were in the foxhole. Didn't you turn to a higher power for guidance?"

I knew exactly what the rabbi was talking about. "October 3, 1951, the National League Championship between the Brooklyn Dodgers and the New York Giants. Bottom of the ninth at the Polo Grounds. Bobby Thompson goes to bat with Brooklyn ahead four to two; two men on base. Ralph Branca throws the pitch and Thompson hits it out of the ballpark — 'The Shot Heard Round the World.' I was listening to Red Barber describe it on the radio and, like every loyal Dodgers fan, that was the worst day of my life. Close to fifty years later, it still ranks up there with the worst."

"Larry, that's sports. Let's talk about reality."

"This *is* real to me. I was saying 'Goddamn it' a lot."

"Aha! So who were you talking to?"

"Myself? Anybody who would listen?"

"But you were talking out loud, right? Who were you talking to? You said 'Goddamn it,' not 'Pee Wee Reese damn it' or 'Oscar Levant damn it.' "

"Irwin, it was just a verbal reaction to unpleasant circumstances. If you put your hand on a hot stove, you say 'ouch.' That's not a prayer by any stretch of the imagination."

"I'm using your logic. You are telling me that at the worst moment in your life you cursed out

131

loud when no one was there to hear it. Who were you asking to damn the situation?"

"It's just an expression."

"A very meaningful expression. Why do you think you were saying this curse?"

I couldn't answer.

"How did you feel after saying the curse?" the rabbi persisted.

"I guess I . . . I felt better."

"There was a change, right? The curse helped you face the issue and, more to the point, it was natural. We can't call that a prayer, but wasn't it an acknowledgment of a higher power? Weren't you hoping that God would intercede? After all, you could have said nothing."

I didn't say anything. I didn't know what to say.

Under certain circumstances profanity provides a relief denied even to prayer.
— MARK TWAIN

IN AUGUST 1986, David Crosby walked out of a Texas Penitentiary in Huntsville, Alabama, after serving five months on a drug and weapons charge.

The celebrated rhythm guitarist for The Byrds, as well as Crosby Stills Nash and Young, had reached the end of his rope. He was addicted to alcohol and cocaine, spending as much as $600,000 a year to support his habit. Actually, David Crosby was passed out in the courtroom when the judge sentenced him to jail. He woke up behind bars.

Going off alcohol and drugs cold turkey in prison was difficult, but David Crosby's greatest challenge was waiting for him when he regained his freedom.

I know I prayed in prison, but I was more frightened than I was sincere. It was something along the lines of "help me" and "this is so terrible" and even then I didn't think of it as a real prayer.

My real prayers started when I got out of prison and was in a twelve-step program. My sponsor kept telling me prayer could help, when I would tell him how tough it was to stay straight. I was doing it, I wasn't drinking, but it was so unbelievably hard because I had been the exact opposite for twenty years.

I told him I felt completely awkward about trying to pray to somebody or something — although I had a notion there must be a higher power; I just hadn't a clue what or who it might be. But I was willing to try it because, at that point, I was willing to try anything to remake myself as a human being.

David Crosby said his first prayer as he looked up at a majestic evening sky out in a field near his home in Marin County in northern California. He looked up to the moon and the mountains and said these words:

Okay, I don't know if there's anybody out there listening, but I'm trying to do the right thing finally and I'm having a terrible time with this. So, I'm not going to ask for things because I've had things. I need some strength. I don't want anything material and I don't even ask for success. I just want more strength so I can do this one thing.

Crosby would say these words over and over again every night. And, slowly, the urge to drink lessened. Today, more than ten years since that first prayer, Crosby is straight. He told us that organized religion is not for him, but there is a comfort he had never had before when he prays.

On November 2, 1994, David Crosby was admitted to the UCLA Medical Center with a failing liver. Although he no longer drank, his body had been worn down by twenty years of alcohol and drug abuse. The doctors told him he needed a liver transplant or he would die.

Lying in the hospital before the transplant, David Crosby's wife, Jan, gave him the news that she was pregnant. But that wasn't all. She also introduced him to a young man, James Raymond — his son from a previous relationship — who had been put up for adoption at birth.

David Crosby had a lot on his mind, in addition to the transplant, when the doctors administered the anesthesia.

I knew I was close to dying and I don't want to snivel, but I came through it with a lot of help. One person gave up his life to save four of us that night by signing his organ donor card. I got a liver and others got a pancreas, a heart, and kidneys. Four people were saved by a fifth signing his name.

I was lying there with all these thoughts and I remember thinking about my contemporaries that had done what I had done, and the fact they were dead and I wasn't. I prayed to God to let me live. I didn't bargain because you gotta be who you truly are and say what you truly need and I don't think bargains reflect that. My words were few:

> *"I don't know what you want, but if you want me to go, well then I'm going to do just that. But if you can see your way clear to let me live, I've got some music to make and some children to raise here and I'd sure love to have the chance to do it."*

I think honesty and simplicity are the key factors. Today my son has joined me in a band. He's a better musician than I am. I have the opportunity to play my guitar for my little son Django. I look at him and think what an incredible jolt of life force he has brought into our lives.

I had to fight my way back to health again and I did it, and I am a lucky man. There are moments when I'm just looking at my son between my wife and me, and then I look at them both and I say to myself, "I'm so damn lucky." And then I say "thank you." And if there ever was prayer, that is it.

When word spread about the famous guitar player's illness, his publicist, Elliot Mintz, told his fans to send prayers. Crosby came through the surgery just fine and is the first to say that, while he isn't an expert on the subject, he believes the prayers from his fans helped.

I'd like to think they did. When I run into people and they tell me, "You know, I was praying for you when you were dying," I tell them thank you, and I believe that stuff works. Or, I'd like to believe it. Who really knows? I have no way to prove it but, when you think about it, I don't have to prove it. I can believe in whatever I want and it suits me to believe it does work.

I was on the computer on the Internet, getting e-mail by the hundreds, and I was getting armfuls of letters three or four times a day. The hospital was swamped and they were almost all good wishes and prayers. Now, again, I can't prove it, but I like to think this works.

David Crosby is now touring with his son in a band called, interestingly enough, CPR — although he claims it has nothing to do with the work of medical technicians. Instead, it is based on last names of the members: Crosby, Pevar, and Raymond.

After the interview he handed over the words to a song that he and his son had written together called "At the Edge." He says that if a song can be a prayer, this is his.

> **Our grasp is fragile**
> **the thread is so thin.**
> **I wonder each day if I'm blowing away**
> **I know that I'm lucky**
> **I wouldn't be here at all**
> **if somebody's hand hadn't been where**
> **I stand**
> **at the edge of a very great fall.**
> **— "AT THE EDGE," WORDS AND MUSIC**
> **BY DAVID CROSBY, JEFF PEVAR,**
> **AND JAMES RAYMOND**

NOVELIST TOM ROBBINS told us that every time he said a foxhole prayer it has been answered, without exception. Sometimes a foxhole prayer is said for a friend.

I remember very late one night, probably two o'clock in the morning, I received a phone call from someone I cared about very much who was in a bar about four or five miles away and in a very troubled state. I knew I needed to get to that person as quickly as possible, but I was very poor at the time and my car hadn't started in more than a month. I thought it was completely dead.

But I got up and dressed anyway, and I went out to the car and I prayed that it would start. The engine turned over right away, it started, and I made my way to the bar and rescued my friend. The car never started again.

ANTHONY ROBBINS is the king of infomercials. He is known as a success coach, and has worked with the crew of America³, Andre Agassi, and the L.A. Kings, among others. Through his motivational audio series *Personal Power II* and his success seminars, Robbins has helped individuals and teams discover their peak performance capabilities. He has written bestsellers such as *Awaken the Giant Within* and has been a guest on my television show.

We interviewed Anthony Robbins by phone one Sunday morning as he sat at his home in Fiji, where it was almost midnight. My first question was, "Do you pray your infomercials will do well?" His answer: "If I prayed every time an infomercial was on, I would have to pray twenty-four hours a day."

But he prays before every seminar, asking God to use him for a greater good. During one of his seminars on the big island of Hawaii, Anthony Robbins had to do some overtime praying. A major part of Robbins' seminar curriculum is strenuous physical activity — to help the attendees overcome personal fears, and to foster teamwork and trust.

One of the seminar attendees fell during one such activity.

It was during the lunch period and I heard the roar of the crowd outside. I saw a man lying on the ground. We have an activity in which you climb a pole. Well, it turns out this man, Howard, failed to note on his form that he had a heart condition and was taking nitroglycerin. Anyway, Howard climbed the pole, had a heart attack, and fell.

I rush out there and clear people away. We had an emergency technician on scene and he's working on the guy trying to revive him. We had people from sixty-one countries attending this seminar, from all religious persuasions and every walk of life, standing right there. I yelled for everyone to back off and let the technician work. "Let's find this man's family and say a prayer."

Howard is turning gray. Twenty minutes have gone by and the hospital crew still hasn't arrived. It took forty minutes before the ambulance arrived. The EMTs finally show up and use the defibrillator that shocks the heart to start it beating. At this point Howard is even grayer. After ten minutes, one of them says to me, "That's it, he's gone."

They start putting Howard into the back of the ambulance. They said to do any more is a waste of time, he's gone, he's flat-lining. I said, "You are not giving up on this man." A doctor who's attending the seminar tells me, "You are wasting your time and there's nothing that can be done. The man has been dead for forty-five minutes." The technician is screaming at me, "This guy is dead, you killed him."

I get another doctor who is attending the seminar to come with me and we are in the ambulance screaming full blast through the island, heading to the hospital, and Howard is not responding at all. Then we took a corner pretty sharp and the defibrillator rolls over, hits the wall of the ambulance, and stops working.

I said to myself, "Oh, my God." I started to cry and then I started praying, because I didn't believe this was Howard's end. By now we're at a point on the island where we are out of radio contact so we can't even talk to the hospital for instructions. I kicked the defibrillator and said, "This is ridiculous." The thing comes back on.

So we keep working on Howard, and four minutes out I remember saying, "Look at him! There's a tiny bit of color!" And then on the monitor the line isn't flat but has a bit of movement. By the time we reach the hospital, thirty minutes after we left, Howard has a bit of a pulse. I wait for ninety minutes before a doctor comes out and takes me to see

Howard. He opens his eyes, looks at me, and says, "What are you doing on my vacation?"

I go back to the seminar — I've been away for almost four hours — and I see the doctor who told me I was wasting my time. I announce that Howard is fine and the doctor calls me a liar. The next day, the doctor asks to speak. He says he trains EMTs and everyone is told that if a patient flat-lines for fifteen minutes, the patient is gone.

He breaks into tears. He says he went to the hospital to prove Howard was dead and he says, "He's alive." The doctor is crying, thinking about all the people that died that now he thinks he could have saved.

I still get a letter from Howard every Thanksgiving.

He doesn't climb poles anymore?

No, he doesn't.

On reflection, was it your persistence or the group prayer, or was it a combination?

Who am I to say? I personally think that the group prayer got him through it. You can't put that many hearts and minds and spirits together and think it could hurt. But I now think it was a combination of us doing our part and God choosing that it wasn't his time. But if we hadn't done our part, Howard would have been gone.

MY FRIEND Cal Thomas lives with his wife,

Ray, in Alexandria, Virginia, close to the Potomac River. They have a beautiful home. In Cal's den is a framed poster of The King — Elvis Presley, that is — an original Coke machine, a big sign announcing "Reagan Country" and, best of all, a Seeburg Selectomatic juke box filled with 45s. I was ready to proclaim Cal's den heaven if that Seeburg had some Slim Gaillard.

After our earlier phone call, I visited Cal to talk in more depth about prayer. Cal told me that the story of his life was a remarkable example of the first half being run by him, with great disaster, and the second half being run and led by God.

In the early '70s, Cal was a respected newscaster for NBC Radio in Washington, D.C., making frequent television appearances to discuss current events, being invited to all the important Washington parties, and he and his wife, Ray, were raising a terrific family. It all ended abruptly.

One of my lowest points was when I was working for NBC in 1973. If you ever work for NBC on a Friday afternoon and the boss says, "You got a minute?" it's all over.

At that time I was thirty years old and I had set that year, from when I was eighteen, as part of a twelve-year plan. I worked hard at it and I had professional and educational goals. Every year on my birthday I'd look back at the previous twelve months.

142

And then the very year I had picked to become a success — I was doing seven network radio newscasts a week, appearing on television, people were starting to recognize me and I'm getting invited places, my name is appearing in the paper — I got canned. I'll never forget it: March 17, 1973, 3:00 P.M., in Washington, D.C.

I walked into a room and it looked like the Grand Inquisition. All of those people in that room are now either dead or out of the business, I might add, but here I am. That was a low point. People I thought I knew well wouldn't return my phone calls. I couldn't find a job and I had to move back to Houston where I'd come from. I took a $20,000 pay cut, we sold both our nice cars, moved to a smaller house with a lesser lifestyle.

It might have looked like a disaster, but two important things happened: I made a commitment to Jesus Christ and there was a total reorganization of my priorities. Until that time I was a nodding acquaintance of Jesus'. I'd go to church and drop some money and that was it. It's like the difference between sandlot baseball and the major leagues.

That night my wife said to me, "You know you'll never be free of this burden of being a success until you thank God for losing your job."

I had three young kids to support. I remember going to the unemployment office where I

143

had covered stories as a journalist before and now I was taking a number. I sat down with a truck driver who had mud on his boots and for whom I wouldn't have had the time of day. But that day we were equal — we didn't have jobs. Out of all this came a tremendous peace. God knew what he was trying to do with me.

There are two kinds of people: those that say to God "Thy will be done." And those to whom God says "OK, have it your way."

— C. S. LEWIS,
THE SCREWTAPE LETTERS

CHUCK COLSON had resigned from his job as special assistant to President Nixon in August 1973 after Nixon's reelection. He thought he had escaped Watergate. He was working on a project for Raytheon's chief executive officer, Tom Phillips, and noticed a change in the CEO's manner.

Tom Phillips was a witness to me. He invited me to his home one night and I went to see him because I was curious about how he had made such a dramatic turn in his own life. He gave me a book written by C. S. Lewis — Mere Christianity — and it was that night, as I was in my car leaving his driveway on the way to pick up my wife, that I couldn't drive. I was crying. That was when I became a Christian.

One month later, the Watergate scandal nabbed Colson and he was brought before a grand jury. In 1974 he pleaded guilty to handing an FBI file on Daniel Ellsberg to the Copley News Service and was ordered to Georgia's Maxwell Federal Prison.

On the day I was sentenced I prayed with my prayer group in a little room just outside the judge's courtroom. I did pray something like "save me" and "get me out of this thing." People pray to be delivered from experiences they don't want to go through. I think it's human nature. And yet it was a good thing he didn't answer that prayer because the best thing that happened to me in my life was when I got out of prison.

I remember in the courtroom the judge saying "one to three years" and I was just shocked. Your heart sinks. I heard the gavel hit and my wife gasp behind me. A piece of your life is taken away. I prayed out on the courthouse steps that I would be a witness in the face of it all.

Tell me about jail.

It's a chilling experience to come out of high government office and go to jail, because half the guys in prison are very happy to kill you. In fact, one tried to do just that. I prayed for my family. It was the lowest point in my life. My prayers were, "Get me through this, help me out here, and, if not, take care of my family." I think prayer, by its nature, keeps you from being self-centered because it is God who brought you into existence and it is God to whom I was praying.

While Colson was in prison, his son was arrested for marijuana possession. Today, Colson sees this as the answer to his foxhole prayers.

It turned out to be a great thing in his life because it got him straightened out. It also ended up that the judge knew about it and cut my prison sentence short. I've always wondered if it took my son getting into trouble for me to get out of prison or, for that matter, my getting into trouble to straighten him out.

You have to know, during those months in prison I was praying consistently that God would show himself to me because I was feeling so desperate. You feel so alone. One day, after that prayer, I got a call from one of the prayer group members saying he was going to meet with President Ford and would ask if he could trade places with me and serve the rest of my sentence.

When I hung up the phone I knew I had seen God's presence, and was free from that moment on. The meeting with President Ford never took place, but a few weeks later I was out on a reduced sentence of seven months.

Colson's time in prison was not wasted. He witnessed firsthand the lack of spiritual assistance available to prison inmates. After his release, Chuck Colson started Prison Fellowship Ministries.

Sometimes you feel a deep conviction about something and it's very clear that's what God wants you to do. When I started this ministry I prayed for God's will. There are some amazing stories that force me to say, "This isn't the way the world works — there has been divine intervention." For instance, when we began we couldn't get into the prisons. We couldn't find any way. Finally, Senator Harold Hughes got me an appointment with Norman Carlson, the head of the Federal Bureau of Prisons.

I told him his prisons were poorly run. Would he be willing to let us take a man out and show him what we could do that the prison couldn't? He said, "Let me ask you a question. Two weeks ago I was in a federal prison in California and a chaplain and an inmate prayed for me and my wife. Why did he do that?" I told him he was prayed for because we are supposed to pray for those in authority and that he loved him.

Less than a minute later he said, "Mr. Colson, I am going to give you permission to go into prisons and take inmates out." I believe the prayer of that inmate back in California was answered.

Colson says every prayer is answered.

Keep in mind that the answer isn't always the one you want. After all, it's God's will, not

147

your will, that is the issue.

Chuck Colson is a recipient of the Templeton Prize for Progress in Religion for his work with Prison Fellowship Ministries. He has testified before Congress on the issues of religious freedom in prisons, and lectures throughout America on the correlation between religious observance and successful prisoner rehabilitation.

ANN RICHARDS, the former governor of Texas, has a razor-sharp wit and can nail an issue in one sentence. After her keynote speech at the 1988 Democratic Convention in Atlanta — where she declared that President George Bush was born on third base and thought he hit a triple — she had every television producer in America trying to book her for an appearance the next day.

We sat down for a conversation with Ann Richards last autumn and she told us a chilling tale about the rough-and-tumble world of Texas politics.

Richards has wrestled with a few demons in her own time, and she talked to us about how those demons came back to haunt her in a couple of election campaigns and how she used prayer to see her through it.

Strength is what I pray for. It's never "God please alleviate my situation" or "Take away the difficulty I am facing." It's always for strength to deal with it on my own.

During one of my races for Texas state treasurer, and in my race for governor, I revealed that I am an alcoholic. Questions were raised about my treatment. Could it happen again? Opponents were also suggesting I was mentally ill. They took my alcoholism and tried to spin it into something they thought would sound worse.

So I prayed for strength during those times. It was very important and it took place during the lowest ebb of my life. I really thought my career was over.

I had been in Alcoholics Anonymous, where you have to give yourself over to a higher power. I had always hedged on what that higher power was, but the AA counselors really brought me up short, saying, "Face up to it! Stop trying to intellectualize it! Give up and give over!" And when I did that, there was a tremendous release.

And so, during political campaigns, which were extremely difficult, I was able to crawl into what I call the core of my being. It's a place that is very directly related and connected to God. During all the charges of being mentally ill and on drugs and being a drunk, I would get into bed at night, close my eyes, and crawl into that core. That connectedness allowed me to do what I was praying for all along: to carry me through a very difficult time.

TODAY, DR. CECIL MURRAY runs the AME Baptist Church — with more than two million members and seven thousand congregations throughout the world — from the mother church in Los Angeles.

But at age twenty-eight he was a radar intercept officer for the air force, based in Oxnard, California. He was assigned to a two-seat F-89 Scorpion jet fighter with William George Burbage of South Carolina.

One morning, on a routine training mission, disaster struck.

I was strapped into the cockpit when the nose cone exploded on takeoff. I said right there, to the Lord, "Hold me." The Lord settled me down so I could take off the parachute and the life jacket, unbuckle the seat belt, place my head in the tiny opening in the canopy, and pull myself out backwards to get out of the burning aircraft.

That was foxhole prayer, and it comes from sheer necessity and trauma. I think the words were some form of hosannah, which means hope in the Lord. It reduces us to utter childhood or child-likeness but not childishness. It knows. It is about some power out there that we know can help us.

William George Burbage, the pilot, a young, white adult from South Carolina, died a month after the crash. His foot had slipped and he fell back into the flames. I heard him call, I rolled him over and extinguished the

150

flames, but he died.

It brings up the question why some prayers are answered with a "yes" and others with a "no" and still others with a "wait." I was spared and he was not and the only rational answer is that I must live for two. There is no rational explanation. There is salvation of your sanity by feeling that when life closes a door, God opens a window. Life closed a door for George Burbage and God opened a window of eternal life for him.

Cecil Murray says the airplane crash was a catalyst in making him turn to religion. He paused for a moment and then told us it's wrong to think ill fortune is sent by God. Instead, he says, life may put ill fortune on us or society may do it, but God, through prayer, will lift it off.

One night I dreamed I was walking along the beach with the Lord. Many scenes from my life flashed across the sky. In each scene I noticed footprints in the sand. Sometimes there were two sets of footprints, other times there was only one.

This bothered me because I noticed that during the low periods in my life, when I was suffering from anguish, sorrow or defeat, I could see only one set of footprints, so I said to the Lord, "You promised me, Lord, that if I followed

151

you, you would walk with me always. But I have noticed that during the most trying periods of my life there has been only one set of footprints in the sand. Why, when I have needed you most, have you not been there for me?"

The Lord replied, "The years when you have seen only one set of footprints, my child, is when I carried you."

— "Footprints in the Sand," Mary Stevenson

Chapter Six
In Sickness and in Health

In June 1997 I went to see my cardiologist, Dr. Wayne Isom.

I had a subtle pain in my shoulder. My doctor gave me the news: An artery in my heart was clogged, and I needed angioplasty as soon as possible. I had been through angioplasty before, plus quintuple heart bypass surgery, so I had a good idea what I was going to face.

Angioplasty is a method of inserting a catheter into the groin, feeding it through your body to the chest, and then opening the clogged artery with a balloon-like device to remove the blockage. It's not the way I would choose to spend a day, but my father died of a heart attack at the age of forty-four and I'm sixty-four, so you accept the hand you've been dealt.

The night before the procedure my fiancée, Shawn Southwick, invited some close friends to our New York hotel suite. Shawn is a devout Mormon and she led the group in a prayer for a successful surgical outcome. Shawn knows I don't pray, but rather than try to change each other, we respect our differences.

When Shawn gathered the group in a circle for the prayer, I joined the circle holding hands and bowed my head out of respect. Now don't start jumping to conclusions — I'm still in neutral, but I hope to hell that Shawn is in drive. And I did feel at peace after that prayer.

The angioplasty went fine and a week later I was back at work. I didn't think much about the prayer after the surgery. I placed my trust in Dr. Isom and the miracles of modern medicine.

After that, Shawn and I started making plans for a September 6 wedding. The wedding was to be a garden ceremony at the Beverly Hills home of my close friends Norm and Mary Pattiz. The reception was to be catered by Wolfgang Puck and we sent out invitations to all our friends. The icing on the cake was to be a week-long honeymoon in Paris. It was a great time in my life. I was in love.

On September 4, two days before the wedding, I was having a quick physical checkup at UCLA Medical Center. More bad news: Another artery was clogged. In just two days I was to marry the most beautiful woman in the world, and instead of the wedding we had to make plans to return to New York for more surgery.

Shawn and I were married in my hospital room in Los Angeles on September 5 at 6:00 A.M., and an hour later I was on a private jet to New York where I underwent another successful angioplasty surgery. While I was recuperating in the hospital, Rabbi Katsof stopped by for a visit.

"How are you, Larry?"

"I'm fine, Irwin. Just sorry that Shawn didn't get her wedding day. All the plans, the arrangements — shot down by a clogged artery."

"You've been doing a lot of thinking about it, haven't you?"

"Irwin, I would be lying if I said I wasn't a little worried, but it is a rather simple surgical procedure."

"Thank God for that."

"I thank Dr. Isom and modern medicine for that."

"Larry, do you see any good coming out of this experience?"

"Good? In three months I've gone through a heart procedure twice. I admit I've been sneaking some chocolate now and then, but the one day I wanted to be perfect turns out to be a disaster. And you're asking me about good? Are you crazy?"

"Just try it. If you had to look at the disaster and say 'this, too, is for the good,' what would you say?"

"I'm alive. I still have the best job in the world and I am married to the most wonderful woman in the world, even if she had to marry me in a dingy, bleak hospital room instead of in the garden where it was supposed to happen."

"Larry, maybe this was a lesson."

"You mean God did this to get my attention?

Why would God want to clog my artery? What have I ever done to God? Did God clog my artery because I won't pray?"

"God didn't clog your artery, you did. Too much rich food, too much cholesterol, who knows? I'm a rabbi not a doctor."

"I won't apologize for enjoying the pleasures of life."

"God doesn't ask that. He wants you to enjoy life, to taste all the fruits the world has to offer. He will hold you responsible for every fruit that you don't taste in this world. Physical pleasure is only the appetizer. The artery is a sign you're out of balance."

"I'm in no mood to banter today, Rabbi."

"Okay. Just one thought and then I'll let you rest. Life is not the be-all and the end-all. The body dies but the soul survives. The pain we feel at death is determined by the extent to which we lived our life as a body or as a soul. If you don't realize you are a soul, death is a painful and frightening experience. If you live life as a soul, then you realize you are just moving from one stage to another."

A man is very ill and asks his rabbi to have the synagogue pray that he will recover. "If you do this, Rabbi, and if I get well, I'll give the synagogue two million dollars. I really need to get better." The prayers are said and the man comes home from the hospital, cured. A few

days later, the rabbi visits and reminds the man of his promise about the two million dollars. "Gee," the man exclaims, "I must have been really sick!"

AS YOU hold this book, numerous studies are being conducted throughout the world on the effect of prayer in connection with health. In 1982 and 1983, a ten-month survey was conducted at San Francisco General Hospital on 393 cardiac patients, using intercessory prayer — one half had prayers said for them while the other half were given no prayers.

Those who did not receive prayer showed a higher incidence of needing antibiotics as well as assistance in breathing. The results of the survey were published in a medical journal in 1988 and immediately started a lot of talk in the medical and spiritual communities.

This study caught the eye of a young doctor named Larry Dossey and sparked his scientific curiosity as to what role prayer played in the healing process. He claims this celebrated study was the genesis of his three books on the subject: *Healing Words*, *Prayer is Good Medicine*, and *Be Careful What You Pray For*.

Dr. Dossey was first drawn to the subject by an incident he witnessed almost twenty years earlier at Parkland Hospital in Dallas, Texas.

I took care of a man who was dying of lung cancer, in 1967 during my first year as a phy-

sician. He had cancer in both lungs and wanted no therapy. He wanted to go home and die. But members of his church showed up all the time and prayed like nuts for him. I wasn't too impressed and didn't give it much thought. I discharged him and forgot about him. He was going to die. I could see it.

A year later I got a phone call from a doctor saying, "You ought to stop by and see your old patient. He's here with pneumonia." I was stunned. I went to see him and looked at his current chest x-ray and there was no evidence whatsoever of his lungs having cancer.

How do you think prayer works in healing?

I don't know how prayer works, but I am fascinated by the theories being put forth by extremely serious, well-respected scientists. Here's where I think we are headed with the explanation: it's no longer suitable for scientists to simply say God did it. That may satisfy laypeople, but we want to know more.

Many scientists, including a number of Nobel Prize-winners, are saying we are going to have to rethink the nature of consciousness. We are going to have to get consciousness out of the brain where we've locked it up and allow it to have effects at a distance, such as we see in prayer.

Dr. David Chalmers, a mathematician of cognitive science, published a landmark theory in December 1995 called "The Puzzle of Conscious Experience." Dr. Chalmers says that it's time to bite the bullet and declare consciousness fundamental in the universe, not derived from anything else, but perhaps on a par with matter and energy. This kind of talk was unheard of ten years ago.

The basic picture coming out of all this is that consciousness can act in the world outside the body, even at a distance. This is what we see in intercessory prayer. It may seem sterile to people who want to ally prayer with a personal God — one is free to do that if one wishes. What scientists are trying to come up with is a theoretical picture which might allow that, if God is part of that picture, people are free to grab it.

You say your work isn't new, it's been going on for centuries. What do you mean by that?

I suspect that Herbert Benson at Harvard is right when he says human beings are hard-wired for reaching out to the idea of something greater than themselves — which we call God. I think it is probably programmed into our biology to look beyond ourselves.

There has never been a culture discovered that does not have some form of prayer, so it seems to be part and parcel of the human condition to want to pray. I don't think people need science to prove that this stuff works. I certainly don't want to say that prayer needs science to validate it. People test prayer every day in their own lives, which is the most important laboratory of all.

159

I think, whether we like it or not, science is a huge factor in our culture, and if science says something works, then that's a very persuasive comment. I, for one, having looked at the evidence, believe that if we can bring science and religion together we will all be better off. And I think we can. The whole idea that we have to keep science and spirituality and prayer apart is an idea whose time has come and gone.

Is it a particular kind of prayer that seems to work? One said aloud or one said in silence?

I'll give you my subjective opinion. I don't think it makes a damn bit of difference how people pray, so long as they are praying with a sense of love and compassion and caring and empathy, and it comes from the heart. They can stand on their heads upside down, chant, dance, be quiet, involve words or go beyond words. I do not believe the external form or behavior of prayer is important so long as it feels genuine and authentic while doing it.

It seems to me that the particular image that we form in our minds of the Absolute or the Almighty is not crucial to prayer. I think this is vitally important to recognize. We can say, on the basis of the studies done, that prayers — of a broad variety of religious beliefs — are effective. And this says something important to our society about the need for religious tolerance.

160

There is no experimental proof that any-body, in any religion, of any idea of God, has a monopoly on prayer. I know this point of view will infuriate a lot of people who think they have captured the market on prayer, but if you look at the evidence you can't defend that conclusion.

Three years ago, only three U.S. medical schools taught courses in religious and spiritual issues; there are now nearly thirty. Eighteen medical schools have received $25,000 grants to sponsor courses on spirituality.
— *JOURNAL OF THE AMERICAN MEDICAL ASSOCIATION* (SEPTEMBER 3, 1997)

DR. DALE MATTHEWS, associate professor of medicine at Georgetown School of Medicine, has been teaching doctors about spirituality for six years and has just published his first book on the subject, *The Faith Factor*. When Dr. Matthews was a professor at the University of Connecticut Medical School, he gave a well-publicized series of lectures on the relationship between faith and medicine, and he says he began to attract a lot of patients who wanted a doctor interested in medicine and the spirit.

Most doctors are trained to take care of diseases, as opposed to taking care of people who happen to have diseases. Seventy-two percent of Americans say that religion is the most important influence in their life.

When I started out in medicine, I said to myself, "If I'm a doctor taking care of patients, I've got to pay attention to all aspects of the patient's experience, and since religion is very important to my patients, I should pay attention to the spiritual needs of my patients."

Patients came to me and said, "I'm here because you are a Christian doctor and I'd like for you to pray for me." When I first heard that, I was flabbergasted. I had never prayed with a patient.

Do you remember that first patient?

Yes, I do. It was an interesting situation. This guy who came to see me not only had a Christian doctor but he had a Christian accountant and a Christian garbage collector and resided in a really rigid world. Everyone else was unclean. And I felt really uncomfortable about this because I was in a state school. It wasn't a life-threatening condition, it was a routine physical. Well, I went through the motions and was glad when it was over.

In 1988, at the University of Connecticut, I started praying more and more and I became more comfortable, not looking around the room hoping nobody else was listening. I decided not only is it okay for me to pray with patients, but it is a good thing for those people who are open to it.

Now, there are risks and benefits. The risk of praying is alienating the patient if they are not interested, so the patient has to be willing. That's one risk. The second one is that it becomes magic, as if the power is in the words you say.

There's a tendency to always look for a formula — if I just say a prayer, or maybe I didn't say the prayer right, or maybe it should have been a rosary or the Lord's Prayer — and that gets you into magical thinking, as opposed to what I think the best use of prayer is: a model that joins the patient and me together under God.

The vision that I have is that a third person enters the room and it actually places the patient and myself on equal footing. I don't have to play God anymore. I can let God be God. It takes me off the throne.

Both Matthews and Dossey say anyone wanting to enter the medical profession today will be taking classes in spirituality, that we may know how to treat the disease but we have to also know how to treat the human being who has the disease.

THAT IS the job of Reverend Stephen Mann, chaplain at Johns Hopkins Hospital in Baltimore. Like Dr. Dale Matthews and Dr. Larry Dossey, Mann is teaching doctors about the spiritual side of their patients.

What do you say to doctors on the first day of class?

You have some physicians who are people of faith and they want to talk more about it. You have others who are very skeptical and are there to shoot things down, and others who are on the fence. We bring out the research that's been done and say this data is good data. It shows a vast number of patients utilize spiritual resources in dealing with a healthcare crisis. It's inappropriate for a doctor to discount that source of support. Doctors should pay attention to it. Even if they don't believe, their patients do.

When you talk to doctors about prayer, you're telling them what?

That this is one part of the healing process. Spirituality has always been a part, although it got lost in the modern centuries as we focused on high-tech. High-tech isn't the panacea for all our ills. People are still stuck with having to define themselves. We can have people who are alive because of high-tech medicine, but they are saying, "Who am I? What am I?" That's a spiritual process.

Doctors in the future must do what then?

They should get information about a person's spiritual history. It should happen in the dialogue between patient and doctor. We're looking for that more and more so that the physician can have a better idea about the resources available for that particular patient.

We already do it in terms of social history and, as a result, doctors will sometimes call in a social worker.

For example, there was an African-American man who came in and was obviously clinically depressed. He kept telling the treatment team his name was Elijah but his slave name was Leroy. They were thinking the guy believed he was the prophet Elijah and that he must be psychotic.

I talked with him and learned he was a Black Muslim, and part of their tradition is to get a new spiritual name and their given name is designated as their slave name. This information resulted in different medications, a better prognosis, and a shorter stay in the hospital.

What do you say to those who say it's a fad?

We have thousands of years of history of the marriage of healing and spirituality. There were times in history when science went against certain ideologies of the church and doctors got the shaft, which was unfortunate and led to a divide. Because science has become high-tech doesn't necessarily provide meaning to those patients now surviving.

In spirituality it's about meaning. What does this mean? Medicine can't solve it all. It's going to get down to what is the individual going to do with himself.

I ASKED Dr. Larry Dossey if he was concerned about an over-reliance on prayer — about the possibility of someone packaging prayers for, say, prostate surgery or diabetes.

Some of the methods of modern medicine are so powerful that we are not going to give them up in favor of prayer. For example, an appendectomy is the most powerful treatment humankind has ever designed against the potentially fatal disease of appendicitis. I can't imagine there's a prayer practitioner out there whose effectiveness could rival that of an appendectomy. I think, however, we'd be better off if we combined the appendectomy with prayer, or prayer plus insulin for diabetes rather than insulin alone.

I think the wave of the future will not be to rely specifically on prayer or specifically on medication or surgery. Clearly, we are headed toward an integrated approach where we get over our intellectual indigestion about keeping these things separate. We need to get beyond this either/or way of looking at things and say they both work — they are compatible.

There are folks who don't agree. I know my friends in the Christian Science organization think that prayer alone is better. They believe prayer, medication, and surgery interfere with each other. I don't believe that personally. These are going to be interesting issues to confront. There's no way to avoid them, be-

cause of the data. We are going to have to engage these questions about how to use prayer in modern medicine.

I believe prayer is a sending out of vibrations from one person to another and to God. All the universe is in vibration.
— NORMAN VINCENT PEALE
THE POWER OF POSITIVE THINKING

I KNEW we had to interview a Christian Scientist, but I was somewhat hesitant about having the discussion because, quite frankly, I think people who won't avail themselves of modern medicine are a little wacko.

But after the interviews with Dr. Dossey, Dr. Matthews, and Reverend Mann, I was having to rethink my position on prayer and medicine. I'm rethinking a lot of positions these days.

So we made an appointment with Virginia Harris, chairperson of the Christian Science board of directors.

What is Christian Science? How does it work? Can you explain it to me?

I'll try. First of all, I feel and believe that the Divine, God, embraces the human, loves the human. To me that's a given. The second given is that God is all power, that God is all presence, that God is all action. As one prays, the prayer is aligning one's thoughts to God, to good, to this all-power. As one does that —

167

this is the how — it changes the way you think. It begins to make you look for the good that is at hand. As one begins to do that, it multiplies.

"It" is the power, the good, the God force behind it. It is the power which then begins to take over your thinking, your consciousness. All the negative thoughts — the fears, the doubts, the distrust, whatever might be causing the physical pain, or frustration about business, anxiety about a relationship — the promise, the force of the good with which you aligned your thoughts through prayer, begins to supercede the negative. Thoughts of peace, hope, trust, encouragement, expectancy, all of these elements bring the expected result: restored health. That's how it works.

If someone is going to the hospital, how would a Christian Scientist pray for that person?

If someone were going in for a procedure, as a Christian Scientist practitioner I couldn't pray specifically for that case. They already have a professional — the doctor who is going to operate. That would be two of us having the patient and ethics says that you just have one. I could pray for the family, I could pray in a general way, but I could not take responsibility for his case nor could I charge him.

Understood. Give me an example then.

A medical nurse with whom I had a conversation discovered a lump. The doctor said come back in a month and she did and it had enlarged. She found herself in a bookstore looking for something to read that would help with her thoughts. She came across this book, Science and Health, *by Mary Baker Eddy. Someone standing next to the nurse urged her to buy the book and read it. "The first chapter is on prayer — I know it will make a difference."*

The nurse bought the book and read the chapter on prayer, even though she wasn't a Christian Scientist. When she went back to the doctor, the doctor said the lump had shrunk. But he still thought they should do something about it, so they scheduled the surgery in two weeks. The nurse kept reading the book, and when she went back, they did the final x-ray before the surgery and the lump was gone. She was told to get dressed and go home — the surgery wasn't necessary.

She didn't call a Christian Scientist practitioner, she just read the book. It was her thoughts which obviously had a physiological effect on her body.

How did you get involved in Christian Science?

My mother was a Christian Scientist, my father wasn't. I grew up in a home that practiced both. I saw both work. As I grew into an adult, I felt that I was very blessed by seeing both treatments.

I made a decision in my life in 1976, after I

was in an automobile accident. I was taken to the emergency room and the doctors did not think that I would live. There were three or four cars involved and it took them forty-five minutes to get me out of the car, it was so mangled.

Lying there in that emergency room when someone has told you they don't think you're going to live, you think about your three little boys you have at home and you think, "Where is God?" And I thought, "Wait a minute, either God is God, or he isn't, and do I feel that he isn't because of what happened to me an hour ago on that expressway?"

God is powerful, able to heal. The doctors wanted to operate immediately, but my husband and I, as Christian Scientists, decided against it. I felt a conviction that God would heal me. And so we went with that — we called a Christian Scientist practitioner to pray and treat me. In that situation the practitioner could, because I was in the emergency room involuntarily, so it's not a conflict of interest.

The practitioner prayed for me, and in a couple of hours my husband signed the release forms and I was taken home in an ambulance. I had broken ribs and severe internal injuries. There were times in those days when I thought I was dying, but obviously I didn't.

You came back with no medical help?

No medical help. When my husband signed the release, they took the IVs out of my arms and the doctors shook their heads. People said I was crazy.

Tell me about sitting in the car. Did you pray?

I did pray. I prayed very earnestly because I knew there wasn't any other help — it was me and God in that car. I prayed for everyone in the other cars. I said to God, "If the people in the other cars are like me, then everyone here is in need of your help."

I don't recall being in a great deal of pain — the shock, I think — but I was drifting in and out of consciousness, and every time I felt myself slipping away I prayed to stay awake. The pull to let go was so great, and if I did, I didn't have a chance. I just knew it. I was injured but my battle was mental. I had to stay conscious. So when I had a sense of bearing, I prayed.

Virginia Harris is a convincing example of the healing power of prayer. She believes that we have abdicated our personal responsibilities in too many areas of our lives and that it is time we take possession of our own thinking and the governing of our own bodies. She believes we have not even begun to tap the resources of God, or of prayer and its power to heal.

Harris predicts that sixty to ninety percent of the cases currently being treated in hospitals could be healed through prayer. She believes that in the future doctors will handle only ten percent of their current caseload.

There are many opinions about the effectiveness of prayer and healing, but from my personal point of view, if my artery clogs again, I'll certainly appreciate my friends' prayers but my first call will be to Dr. Isom.

THERE WAS one more doctor I wanted to touch base with about prayer and healing — Deepak Chopra, educational director of The Chopra Center for Well Being, in La Jolla, California. Chopra is the best-selling author of *Ageless Body, Timeless Mind*, to name but one of his numerous books and audios.

His pioneering work in the field of mind/body medicine has helped countless individuals achieve success and fulfillment through his unique blend of Western medicine and the ancient health traditions of Ayurvedic medicine. The basic tenet of Ayurveda is that one's physical health is the balanced integration of body, mind, and spirit.

Have you ever prayed for your patients?

Yes, there were many times I prayed for my patients when I was a practicing physician, especially when unanticipated things came up, when something suddenly went wrong. Whenever that happened, I would go to the chapel in the hospital and pray for the patient. I got into the habit of praying every time something went awry, with the understanding "Thy will be done," so that I didn't sound like I was saying that I knew better.

Have you ever seen a direct relationship between prayer and someone's recovery?

To me, there is always a direct relation. I have one very dramatic story, which sounds almost incredible and therefore would be dismissed by scientists. Many years ago a patient in Massachusetts had surgery for a brain tumor. I prayed for her preoperatively and when the surgeons operated they couldn't find the tumor. They found only a little clot of blood.

The fact is that she'd had a biopsy before and this was a recurrence. There are many ways of interpreting that, but when I was told about it, my immediate impression was that somehow the prayer had influenced the tumor, so that it actually died out by the time the surgeons went in. It was a penetrating experience for me.

How do you think prayer works?

Because of my interest in quantum physics, I have wondered about this for a very long time. The idea is to not conceptualize God, because as soon as you conceptualize God, you limit God. A concept is a definition, a label, and any definition of God is then not God because you limit him in the very act of defining him. God is always transcendent and beyond any narrow concept.

Having said that, I do have a certain visual image of the expression of God. I have an image of a transcendent, infinite, eternal, conscious, energy field and I am an expression of, a product of, and contained within, that conscious energy field.

There's a Rumi poem that says, "All my life I've been knocking at the door, and when it finally opened, I realized I was knocking from the inside." So I'm within.

Saint Augustine had an expression, "Behold, you were within me and I outside myself, and there I search for you." My visual impression of God's first expression is this conscious energy field. My own desires, my own intentions, and my own prayers are an impulse in that field.

The field has infinite organizing power and infinite correlation. It can integrate the impulse that I've introduced into it, so long as I'm detached from an outcome. That detachment is necessary because if I'm attached to an outcome then I am trying to influence the field.

But once I've introduced the intention and gotten my personal ego out of the way, then the field, with its infinite organizing power and correlation, organizes space/time events which affect the outcome and infinity. I hope this is comprehensible, but that's how I understand it.

Okay. Let me see. . . . Some people say that prayer is a sign of weakness. What would you say to that?

174

I think that's very arrogant and very bellig-erent. What that is saying is there's me and then there's God out there, and it's me against God. I would say prayer is a sign of humility, and humility signifies strength. It is a sign of self-esteem that your identity is not tied in with your skin-encapsulated ego. That's an illusion.

When you pray, you have actually shifted your internal reference point from your ego to your spirit. The spirit is the domain of your awareness, where you experience universal-ity. The ego is the domain in which you expe-rience self — where you wallow in self-pity.

Most people are confused between self-image and self-esteem. The self-image is an internal reference point and it's based on object referral, which means we refer to situa-tions, circumstances, people, and events in order to identify ourselves. If you meet some-body on the street and ask who he or she is, I don't think the usual response is going to be, "I'm a holographic expression of unbounded consciousness, which is manifesting a space/time event in a field of infinite probabilities." A more likely answer would be, "I'm a banker."

Our concept of who we are is really so lim-ited. We must come to the prayerful realiza-tion that we are a powerful expression of unlimited, eternal intelligence.

What about the importance of will?

When I hear the word "will," I understand it

as the will of God — which says that if I could align myself, have the experience of atonement or atunement, then thy will and mine will be the same. That has profound strength. It's like a mighty tidal wave. My personal will is an illusion, a figment of my imagination. As I see it, surrendering to the mystery of existence and the mystery of God, and aligning ourselves with the will of God, is the only kind of will that ultimately works.

Look to your health; and if you have it, praise God, and value it next to a good conscience.

— IZAAK WALTON
THE COMPLEAT ANGLER

SENATOR ORRIN HATCH was terrified when he woke up one morning in 1996 and couldn't hear out of his left ear. The four-term Republican senator from Utah had no inclination anything was wrong when he had gone to bed the night before. After waiting a few hours to see if this was a temporary problem of some kind, Senator Hatch went to the Bethesda Naval Hospital just outside Washington, D.C., for a full battery of tests.

The doctors had narrowed down the problem — either it was a tumor and Senator Hatch faced a twenty-one-hour operation with no promise of being able to hear again, or he had a virus which had already destroyed his hearing in that ear altogether. The doctors finally ruled out the tumor when an MRI showed no abnormal growth around his ear. Further testing didn't tell them much more. Senator Hatch was told that he might regain as much as ten percent of his hearing sometime in the future, but there were no guarantees he would ever be able to hear again.

He received this news on a Friday as he sat alone in his Capitol Hill office. He wondered if this was the end of his political career, which began in 1976 when he defeated the three-term incumbent Democrat Frank E. Moss, carrying fifty-four percent of the vote when all the experts said it couldn't be done.

Senator Hatch picked up the phone and called two Mormon Church priests he knew. He asked them to come to his Capitol Hill office as soon as possible to give a blessing.

The next Monday I still couldn't hear anything, but I had tremendous faith that I was going to be healed. At my staff meeting that morning I couldn't hear anything out of that ear. The meeting concluded, everyone filed out of the room, and I returned to some pressing paperwork. The phone rang, and for some reason — maybe my right hand was busy or something — I put the phone against my left ear. It was Ruth, my executive assistant. We started talking about some issue, when all of a sudden I realized I could

177

hear through that ear!

I dropped to my knees in my office, right beside my desk, and thanked God for this wonderful blessing. I had tears in my eyes. Today I have a rumbling in my ear, like an inner-ear problem, but it doesn't cause me any imbalance or anything. It's just a constant sensation that is always there, sort of like when you're on an airplane that has changed altitude.

Senator Hatch returned to Bethesda Naval Hospital for more tests, and when the doctors were done they all started using the word "miracle." The tests showed he had perfectly normal hearing in his left ear.

I have no doubt in my mind it was a miracle from our Father in heaven. I think the Lord was telling me, "Do my will and I'll bless you, but you've got to start doing my will." I thought I was doing it, but I'll tell you — I've tried even harder since that experience. I know God works in people's lives. I know God can heal people.

OLYMPIC SKATER Scott Hamilton has made a career out of stunning the world with his skills on the ice. He has sixteen championships to his name, as well as a fifth-place finish in the 1980 Winter Olympics held in Lake Placid, New York. In 1984 he won a gold medal at the Winter Olympics in Sarajevo. From there he went on to become one of the country's most popular stars of ice shows, including the Ice Capades.

And then came March 13, 1997. Scott Hamilton stunned the country again — with the announcement from the Cleveland Clinic Foundation in Ohio that he had testicular cancer. Until this moment, his conversations with a higher power had been more of saying "thank you" than a prayer. As a matter of fact, Hamilton never prays before a performance, preferring to wait until after he comes off the ice. He told us what he does is pretty small in the grand scheme of things and he has been given more than he deserves.

As for prayers during his fight with cancer, Hamilton believes the ones coming from other people had more of an effect on his healing than anything he did.

When I was told I had cancer, I accepted it as a kind of destiny thing. I was scared, but I didn't ask for help from God. It's kind of strange, but I thought it must be happening for a reason, and accepted it and did everything I could to beat it.

I was getting cards and letters from people everywhere saying they included me in their prayers. I think it made all the difference in the world. I feel fortunate that I was included in so many people's prayers and best wishes. That kind of positive feeling — of people having faith and believing and giving of themselves — made a differ-

ence in my energy.

There were even small children praying for me every night before they went to bed. I think if you can touch one child, you can touch five thousand, ten thousand people, because that child will pass the deed on.

When you were told that you had cancer, wasn't there a part of you that said, "God, why?"

No. I've had disagreements with God in the past, when my friend Grinkov died at the age of twenty-seven of a heart attack. I was upset and I asked why. I mean, the year before he won an Olympic gold medal with his wife. He was so vital. . . . I just didn't understand why. That was the first time I questioned God in a long time.

I think when something is dealt to you, it's easier for you than for those around you. When you're suffering from a life-threatening illness, it's tougher on the people who love you. It's your challenge and you can focus your energy on fighting it. If you're a bystander, it's really difficult to contribute — you don't know what to do. You're helpless.

When my mother died, I realized how many lives she affected, and how that is passed on to the next person and to the next person. I think any gift given in a selfless way is passed on, always. And if more people would realize that, more people would practice that philosophy and the world would be a better place.

Do you feel God played a role in your success?

Oh, absolutely. I look back now on what I accomplished as a competitive figure skater and there's no way I could have done that on my own. Look at the conviction, the self-discipline, and the determined training — there's got to be something there pushing. What is asked of the body, the mind, and the soul is unbelievable. There has to be some sort of divine intervention.

How much is raw talent? How much is training?

You can teach your body to do anything within reason. It takes will, determination, and discipline to push the memory into the muscle and to shape your body to do the job you're asking it to do. Real will is to dig beyond your limitations. Once you do that, it just comes down to what is meant to be — if you can accept that everything becomes so much easier if you just put yourself in the hands of that higher power.

Hamilton's cancer is gone and he remains convinced that prayer is the reason.

ED KOCH, the former mayor of New York City, once sent me a handwritten letter saying he wanted to come on my radio show and talk about his stroke. He thought that if I talked about my heart attack and he talked about his

181

stroke, together we could save a few thousand people in one night.

That was 1986. Until his stroke, Ed Koch had only prayed in moments of need.

And when he was in an ambulance traveling through Manhattan streets toward a hospital, that was his moment of need.

I was worried I might lose my speech, I might become an invalid or crippled in some sense. And so I did have a conversation — actually it was a monologue, now that I think about it — with God. What I said was, basically, I'd had a full life and I don't mind dying. "If it's your wish to take me now, I have no problem with it."

But I asked God to not engage in salami tactics — don't take me a little bit at a time. And I think he heard my prayers, because I'm in the category of one-third of one percent who have no residual adverse effects of any kind that doctors could find.

Now, when I'm in the hospital, Rabbi Schneier comes in and says, "I'm not going to stay very long because you need to sleep, but I want to urge you to ask for God's intercession by saying the prayers in both Hebrew and English. They are easy, 'Heal me and I shall be healed, save me and I shall be saved.'" I said the prayers and the rabbi was gone.

Then Cardinal O'Connor comes in and he says he won't stay very long because I need to sleep. He says I'm in his prayers, and if I'd like he'll pray for me in Hebrew. I said, "Your Eminence, I already took care of the Hebrew, so could you just do the Latin?"

NOAH WYLE spends a lot of his time in hospitals. He plays Dr. John Carter on the NBC hit series *ER*, which for the past two years has occupied, if not the top spot, then a very respectable placement among the ten most-watched television programs.

Every Thursday night, the writers bring us stories of real crisis and drama at the fictional County General Hospital in Chicago. But there was a time a few years ago when Noah found himself in a hospital and Dr. John Carter wasn't along.

This wasn't television. Noah's grandfather was having triple by-pass surgery.

I started to reevaluate my relationship with him and I saw a lot of ways I had wasted a lot of time and energy trying to manipulate or control how he would perceive me in adulthood. I kept a distance from him. I never asked him for anything or let him have a hand in my success. I guess I wanted to be a success on my own and then show him and be praised as a result.

And then I saw him lying there in a hospital bed, slit from gullet to gizzard, and I realized this is a man I had barely gotten to know and that was because of my standoffishness, of wanting him to respect me. It was a fool's game. I should have been learning from him. I never bothered to ask him a question.

So I prayed right there. I asked that he not die. I asked for a second chance to right what I perceived to be a wrong in how I had been dealing with him. I prayed for strength to carry out this new awareness. I wanted to put to rest all the old baggage and not let anything from the past affect this new light.

Wyle says this was a prayer for a second chance rather than a prayer for time to do more of the same. His grandfather recovered. Today, they have long conversations with each other and there is time for lots of questions from the younger to the older man.

KENNY ROGERS told us about a time when prayer brought his entire family together. As a young boy he went to his grandfather's funeral with his father, but some members of the family weren't able to attend the ceremony. He recalls his father leaning over to him and saying, "That's the one thing in my life that I hope doesn't happen to me. I want to see all of my kids before I die."

My father went into the hospital for what was to be routine surgery. As it turned out, he had complications and the doctors told us he might not make it. Well, my older brother wasn't around, so we went into the hospital room and held hands and said a prayer, asking if there was any possibility our father could last long enough for my older brother to arrive. We knew this was important to my father.

There are eight kids in my family, so this was a major request to have everyone in the same room at the same time. Well, sure enough, my brother gets into town and sees my father and they talk. Two and a half hours later, my father died. It was an absolute answer to a family prayer.

Rogers thinks the prayer was answered because of the biblical axiom about when two or more pray for the same thing God hears it loud and clear.

THERE WAS also an infamous doctor I wanted to talk to about this subject. It was in 1990 that the world first heard about Jack Kevorkian, a retired pathologist from the Detroit area. And with the introduction of Kevorkian came a new phrase: assisted suicide.

Jack Kevorkian took thirty dollars' worth of parts and constructed a machine capable of administering a lethal combination of chemicals into the body at the touch of a button. A patient could push the button to begin the flow of drugs that would administer their own death, or their release, depending on your perspective.

185

It is a subject that has divided the country and, as such, has brought labels from "hero" on one side, to "Dr. Death" on the other. The debate continues: Should a person have the right to take his or her own life if science and medicine can no longer maintain its quality?

Do you pray?

You must have been short of people to have to ask me. I don't pray. When I listen to Bach's music, that's my prayer. That has the same power in my life that religion has in most other people's lives.

Have you ever prayed?

No, I don't think so. I don't know if there's a God and, as a result, prayer seems like psychotherapy. It's all right if that's what you believe in. I don't believe in anyone or any philosophy. I can't say it doesn't exist. I just say I don't know. That's the only honest answer. It makes people feel better.

It's 1990. You are on trial. The jury goes out to deliberate. What's going through your mind?

I'm hoping for a conviction. I want to verify that we are living in the Dark Ages.

Can you tell me about your patients? Did they pray?

I always ask if they want prayers or religious consultation and they all say "no." Most say they have already made their peace with God and have already talked with a priest or a rabbi or a minister, but some say that they just don't want any. I do it to be fair because the person may really want a religious or spiritual consultation but has never had one or is afraid to ask for one. So I bring it up.

What happens when you die?

You rot. You stink for a while and decay and turn into an ugly skeleton. But who knows? What happens when you sleep? There's a philosophy that everything in the world is my universe and my consciousness, because when it's gone there's nothing. And that's a valid concept, but it's so scary and barren that nobody wants to believe it. It's logically and empirically true. If I sleep and don't dream, there's nothing. If I dream, there's a whole different existence than what you see.

So if your consciousness when you are awake and your consciousness when you dream are different, whoa! They have whole different natural laws. You can fly in your dreams, leap mountains, you see grotesque forms that don't exist and ideas you couldn't dream of having when you are awake — that's existence. But when it disappears, there's nothing. No universe, no space, no time, no world, nothing. And this is actually the mystery of life. And you can see why religions were developed.

When others have been around you and have prayed, be it at a wedding or saying grace, what have you done?

I am silent and bow my head. I don't want to embarrass or offend anybody. I don't lose anything by doing that. I don't believe in what they are doing but it's harmless, and silently bowing your head, to me, is the only decent thing to do. Why offend anybody? Why make a scene?

WHEN RABBI KATSOF found out I wanted to include an interview with Dr. Kevorkian he wrote to me asking why.

"Kevorkian stands for everything I am against. Life is precious, every last second, no matter how ill you are. I know this from first-hand experience. I lost my mother four years ago after a very lengthy, courageous, and painful battle with cancer. By the end she was totally incapacitated, in excruciating pain. Sure, we posted on her charts 'do not resuscitate,' but we weren't going to end her life prematurely. She did not want that. By the end, she realized she was only 'will' in a body.

"That is an important lesson in life, perhaps the most important. Life is a series of challenges and how we handle them determines our level of humanity. When a person is free from troubles, they are usually free of growth as well.

"I am enclosing an excerpt from my interview with Dr. Abraham Twerski who lost his wife to cancer. His words illustrate far better than I can the proper relationship to God and death."

I can't understand many things. I can't un-

derstand illnesses, illnesses in children, children born deformed, the Holocaust. There are so many things that are beyond our capacity to understand. Some things were beyond Moses' capacity to understand, and when Moses asked God, "Why are you allowing people to suffer?" God said, "I'm not going to tell you, not as long as you're inhabiting a human body."

And the answer to your question about prayers and my wife's death is yes — I prayed. I thought as hard as I could and realized I'm not the first person to whom this has happened and that I'm sure God had his reasons for doing things that I couldn't understand. I had to be grateful at that point for forty-three wonderful years.

One of the things I said to myself was suppose somebody came up to a husband on the day of his wedding and said, "I'll guarantee you forty-three happy years. Sign on the dotted line." You'd have to be stupid not to sign. So many people don't get that. So, I was given forty-three wonderful years of marriage. Of course I wanted more. You make your peace with that.

Chapter Seven
Prayer and the Big Deal

I do benefits for all religions.
I'd hate to blow the hereafter
on a technicality.
— *BOB HOPE*

My Cardiac Foundation has an annual November fund-raiser to help those who can't afford heart surgery.

I began this charity after seeing the hospital bills following my heart attack and bypass surgery. I was lucky to have insurance, but the size of those bills made me wonder how anyone without insurance could ever afford the proper care.

The Evening with Larry King and Friends is a popular event. We invite over four hundred guests to a Washington, D.C., hotel for dinner, a silent auction, and entertainment featuring stars such as Don Rickles and Michael Bolton.

At the last fund-raiser I was master of ceremonies. Before the program began, I was running through some last-minute details with the technical crew when I heard a familiar voice.

"Larry, got a minute?" It was Rabbi Katsof. I asked the two sound engineers and the cameraman to excuse me for a moment and turned to gaze upon the best-dressed rabbi I had ever seen. He looked good in a tuxedo and I told him so.

"I hope your charity raises a lot of money tonight. I want you to know I said a prayer."

"I would have expected nothing less but I don't think your prayers, expert as they are, will help here. I gotta talk with the technical folks or this whole program crashes and burns and it'll be my fault. I have a lot of cues to hit for this to come off tonight." I looked over at the three engineers who were donating their talent to the evening. Then I cast an eye toward the crowd.

"There are a lot of wheelers and dealers here supporting what we're trying to do," I told the rabbi, "and tonight must be perfect."

"It's a worthy cause, Larry. It's to your credit that you not only recognized a need but that you actually stepped forward to do something about it. Good works are a way of sharing God's wealth and thanking God for the blessings he has bestowed."

"Irwin, these are very successful businesspeople. They give back to the community all the time."

"Why do you think they do it?"

"Who knows. Guilt? The tax write-off? I couldn't say." I was being flip, but I really didn't want to get into anything too heavy before the show. I don't like to rehearse, but I do like to be prepared.

"I think you're underestimating them. I've done a lot of fund-raising. I'll bet if you asked some of *them* you'd get some interesting ideas about prayer."

"Okay, Irwin, next up: businessmen. But right now, I gotta get back to this."

"Keep in mind," he said quietly, "that you may be the master of ceremonies here, but there is a real Master in charge. He can help if you just open your office door." With that, he said goodbye and strolled away.

"Mr. King? You okay?" Robert, the cameraman, looked a little concerned. "That guy bothering you?"

"As much as he can, Robert, as much as he can."

The program went off right on time and I hit every cue. And at the end, as I said good night, I thanked everyone who had helped make the evening a huge success.

Well, maybe not everyone.

A man is praying. He says, "God?"
God says, "Yes?"
The man says, "Can I ask you a question?"
God says, "Go right ahead."
The man asks, "What is a million years to you?"
"A million years is like a second."
The man thinks this over and then

asks, "What's a million dollars
to you?"
God says, "A million dollars is like
a penny."
"Then can I have a penny?"
God says, "Sure, just a second."

MERV ADELSON is chairman of the Beverly
Hills-based East/West Capital Associates, an in-
vestment corporation specializing in media and
software ventures. In other words, he invests in
technology that makes me look better on television. An ambitious goal to say the least.

Adelson knows his stuff. He founded Lori-
mar Telepictures in the 1970s, which was sold
to Warner Bros., which is now part of Time
Warner Inc., where he serves as a member of its
board of directors.

Yes, he is busy. Yes, he prays.

*Every morning and every night. I meditate
in the morning and usually finish with a
prayer. It makes me feel good about myself
and I think, too, prayer sets me up for the day.
I spend about half an hour. I thank God for
everything I have and then I ask for wisdom
in order to live the day in the right way. And
then I say a favorite prayer from Saint Francis
of Assisi:*

*Lord,
make me an instrument of thy peace.*

Vhere there is hatred, let me sow love;
vhere there is injury, pardon;
where there is doubt, faith;
where there is despair, hope;
where there is darkness, light;
and where there is sadness, joy.

Oh, divine Master,
Grant that I may not so much seek
to be consoled as to console;
to be understood as to understand;
to be loved, as to love;
for it is in giving that we receive,
it is in pardoning that we are pardoned,
and it is in dying that we are born to
eternal life.

It's the best thing I've ever found and I've used it for the past ten years or so. It fits. It says all the things I like to say to myself. I pray quietly in my office. I don't pray for anything specific — I have always had this innate belief that I want to say thank you and not ask for stuff — I ask God to give me wisdom and I pray for the health of my family. But I don't pray for this or that to happen.

The essence of prayer is to thank God, to reach God and to create an atmosphere that God wanted us all to have. If we all created that kind of atmosphere, we'd have a different kind of world.

Now, there's another prayer I use every

night and it came from my mother. It comes from somewhere or it's just words she made up — I'm not sure which — but she gave it to me when I was a little kid and I say it before I go to sleep:

Now I lay me down to sleep,
God Almighty care for me.
Please forgive me if I had this day
any wrong in work or play.
Please help me always to do right
and bless me every day and night.

I see God as a giving God, so if you do a decent job of giving then you'll get a decent return on what you give. If what you give is not given with the intent to get it back, then you'll get it back.

What do you think our role is in this world? What's man's job in this world? What's your job? Why are you here?

Well, now you're getting into some deep stuff I really don't want to spend a lot of time with.

One minute?

I think that I am here to correct some stuff that I didn't do in my last lifetime. And I'm here to do a better job than I did the last time around — and evolve. I believe there's more than one lifetime. When it comes time that I haven't anything left to correct, then I won't be here. I'll be someplace wonderful.

Merv Adelson and his wife, Thea, are well-known around Aspen, Colorado, where they host underprivileged children in their home. When you look up the definition of "giving back," you should find the name Adelson.

IF ANYONE has ever faced a Big Deal, it is Sir John Marks Templeton. Now in his eighties and living in the Bahamas, Templeton has more than seventy mutual funds bearing his name. Two of the largest are the Templeton Growth Fund and the Templeton World Fund. When the assets of all the funds are added together, the total exceeds twenty billion dollars. *Wall Street Week* named him to its 1990 Hall of Fame as a result of the Templeton Fund performance. In 1987, he was knighted by Queen Elizabeth in recognition of his philanthropy.

He is the founder of the Templeton Prize for Progress in Religion, a $1.27-million award given every year to a person contributing to the increase in man's understanding of God. He is convinced his spirituality is directly responsible for his financial accomplishments. He is funding research into the intersection of prayer and medicine — testing in a scientific environment the health of those "born again" against a group of atheists. It appears that the "ungodly" seem to have a higher incidence of heart and stomach trouble.

Sir John serves on the board of directors for

The Templeton Foundation, and they plan to spend as much as thirty million dollars every year to finance scientific experiments on spiritual questions.

We interviewed him on a September afternoon when the Dow had jumped more than two hundred and forty points. Sir John didn't know this, which is proof enough that he really did retire in 1992.

I pray to be in tune with God's purposes. Humans are not wise enough to know what is best, and so you pray that what you do and think and say is in tune with God.

I have annual shareholders' meetings for each of the seventy mutual funds with my name, and each begins with a prayer. I've retired from all that now, but this is still done with my son. As an example, we have a shareholders' meeting in Canada which is also beamed by satellite around the world. That's nine thousand people. We begin with a prayer. I've been doing this for fifty years. Now, I cannot say that prayer has caused the good performance of these funds, but maybe it did.

I think everyone can do better and everyone is likely to produce better results if their minds are clear and they are thinking straight. It's important in any activity, especially in managing investments. Focusing on prayer allows you to do this. I think using words, saying it out loud, will clarify your thinking. I say prayers silently and I'm convinced it helps my thinking.

Now, I don't think of the word "hear" when we speak of God and prayer because that suggests God is a person. We are discovering God is larger than humans ever comprehended and so it isn't as if you are talking to another person. We need to bring our human mortality into tune with a more basic reality we don't yet understand. So we need to be humble in thinking we can "talk" to God. It's by no means certain God can "hear" in terms of words.

I think it's much more like we are a tiny part of God in some mysterious way. Maybe there's a similarity in the analogy of a wave on the ocean and our relation to God. A wave is not the ocean, but neither is the wave separate from the ocean. The wave is not eternal and long-lasting the way the ocean is, but the wave and the ocean are related to each other. The God I pray to in those shareholders' meetings is vastly greater than we as humans have conceived as of yet.

John Marks Templeton has written a terrific book called *The Humble Approach*, which suggests that the sooner human beings stop seeing themselves as the centers of the universe, the better off we will be and the sooner we might begin learning more.

ON THE day I spoke with Norman Augustine, vice-chairman and CEO of Lockheed Martin, the Justice Department announced that it had problems with a proposed merger of this aerospace-industry giant with another giant, Northrop, and would oppose the deal on its potential of becoming a monopoly worth thirty-five billion dollars.

Augustine's company employs more than 177,000 people and builds everything from a replacement for the space shuttle to state-of-the-art aircraft to satellites to missiles.

Augustine told me that prayer is part of his life, but he had no words for God about the Justice Department.

I didn't get up and say a prayer for it this morning. I knew it was going to happen and that it was a fait accompli. I try not to bother the Lord with things that will probably work their way out one way or another.

I tend to say my prayers for things that are pretty overwhelming or life threatening. I suspect the Lord is very busy. But if it were a business issue that was threatening the company, like a hostile takeover, I probably would pray. And I have prayed during the waiting for a contract to be awarded. When they are really important to the company and not for personal gain, that's when I'll pray.

The Joint Strike Fighter is a great example — designed for short takeoffs and vertical landings — and there are still two contestants for one slot. My prayer is that we have done all that we know how to do and that we have done our job as well as we could. I pray while we do the bid and I pray when it goes out. I don't want to sound like this is all I do, but there are no atheists in a foxhole.

I am well aware that when I said a prayer for the Joint Strike Fighter contract the CEO of the other company was probably doing the same thing. It's like athletes praying. I think you just pray that you do your best. That's all you can legitimately ask. Everyone can't win.

I remember April 12, 1981, during the launch of Columbia, the first space shuttle. My company makes a major portion of the shuttle and so many people put so much of their lives into it. You watch friends of yours climb aboard — friends with families. You know that very little mistakes can have disastrous consequences, so during the end of the countdown I turn to prayer.

Then, of course, when Challenger blew up I was praying that it wasn't us that caused it. That was a horrible day. Initially it looked like it was a part we built that caused the problem, but it turned out it wasn't. We build the large orange fuel tank for the shuttle and it worked just fine, but in the first few hours that wasn't what we were thinking. That was a bad day for the whole country.

I have a prayer I learned in high school that

I often say: "Let us not be frightened by the problems that confront us but, rather, give thee thanks that thou has given us the opportunity to show our worth. And let us be part of the answers, not problems, of the people of our time."

There was a fraternity at my high school in Denver — that's the fraternity prayer. I thought it was poignant. I've said it a zillion times. I said it that day. I think the most important thing is to say what's on your mind. Be candid, because you can't fool the Lord.

WE ALSO spoke with Ace Greenberg, chairman of Bear Stearns, but it was a brief conversation.

Do you ever pray?

No, I think praying is a mistake. When people are in a crisis they should do less prayer and more action.

You believe in action in a crisis?

God has too many other things to worry about.

Do you believe in God?

Yes, I do, but I don't want to get into that.

So when it comes to the Big Deal, or crisis, your feeling is . . .

Less praying and more thinking.

THERE IS no end to the number of scripts Hollywood has produced and, for that matter, rejected, in which someone prays for a positive turn in an upcoming event such as getting a part in a movie or getting the deal closed or just getting through the day. Art imitates life even in Los Angeles, where it is often considered to be the other way around.

David Sacks, co-executive producer of *3rd Rock from the Sun*, talked to us about his prayers for the smash-hit series before the acclaim. You see, most pilots for TV series never see the light of day.

Each network is pitched between four hundred and six hundred ideas per year. From these they choose about fifty scripts to be written, and from those perhaps twenty-five pilots are shot. Depending on the network's needs, maybe five to eight new shows are then bought, and short orders — six episodes of each — are placed. In the old days, there was at least a firm thirteen, and in some cases as many as twenty-six shows guaranteed.

You've been very successful in the TV industry, David. Has prayer played a role in that?

Being in the entertainment business is like being on a roller coaster. If you know there is a greater reality, a bigger story functioning, it helps keep things in perspective. It helps keep you grounded.

Any time you prayed for help with *3rd Rock*?

I was there on the first official day of production for the pilot. I wasn't a full member of the staff at the time, I was just someone lend-

ing a hand. I looked around and saw dozens of people and I realized most pilots don't go — meaning they end then and there in terms of employment opportunities.

I thought to myself that all of these people are hoping so much that this show will be successful and I realized so many people's livelihoods were at stake, in terms of this show's success. I remember saying a prayer that God would bless this show, just so all these people would have jobs. I feel as though that prayer was answered.

It was answered. In 1996, *3rd Rock from the Sun* star John Lithgow won an Emmy for best actor in a comedy and the NBC series received nominations in two other categories.

I SPOKE with another co-executive producer, Jon Andersen, who, along with his wife, Martha Williamson — whom he met and married while working on the show — is responsible for the very successful CBS series *Touched by an Angel*, on Sunday nights, and *Promised Land*, on Thursday nights.

He says prayer played a major role in the development of *Touched by an Angel*.

Did you pray in the early days of the series?

I wasn't in the picture when the original pilot was done and neither was executive producer Martha Williamson. We were brought in afterwards and asked to do six episodes. The pilot had been called Angel's Attic *and featured dollhouses and miniature people. The camera would take you into the dollhouses where everything became real.*

The audience-testing for the pilot showed that people really liked Della Reese and Roma Downey. Martha thought the show trivialized God and angels, and initially said, "No thanks." But she went home and prayed about the decision, and after some agonizing she concluded that she had to do something. Martha called CBS back and pitched them on doing the show her way.

So how did you become involved?

I was going through a particularly bad time. My son had been killed mountain climbing in British Columbia, my marriage was in trouble, and I was starting to drink too much. Then I got a call from Bob Gros at CBS, who felt I had the necessary experience to partner with Martha who had never before produced an hour-long drama series. So I went to Salt Lake City and met with Martha.

We really struggled during those first days, because money was tight and the industry felt the show was sure to fail. But since I was grieving for my son, I was able to express feelings and experiences that I had bottled up for a lifetime. This was to be of great value to Martha, since the show was about human emotion and I could express a man's point of view.

Martha prayed every day and at one point asked me to join her. I did, but I wasn't comfortable during those first few attempts at prayer. Martha would take my hand and say, "Let's pray." I began to listen. This was difficult and we only had our feelings to rely on as a resource. Her vision was simple: God exists. God loves you. God wants to be a part of your life.

There are a lot of people who want to believe, but there's nowhere to get that kind of information in an acceptable form. Nothing is more powerful than information that comes from TV characters that you love. So during the making of the first six shows we frequently asked God for assistance. "Father, help us with this problem. Help us come to a conclusion about this or that. Help us to keep our minds open for your answers. Help us bring the right person to a particular role."

And did God do that?

Yes. We prayed for that on several occasions that I can think of. One in particular, we had cast John Amos as a powerful father who put great pressure on his son to succeed. The character was merciless and the son finally attempted suicide and ended up in the hospital as a result of the father's pressure. John Amos's character had a meeting with the doctor, who revealed that the son tried to kill himself. The father went into a rage about how his son would never do that.

As the character, John Amos was screaming and finally broke down in tears. John's performance was so real and so powerful. It was truly amazing. Martha and I thought it was some of the most effective dramatic work we had seen in a long time. When we finished, the entire crew was in tears. I found out later that John Amos had a nephew who committed suicide as a result of a tragic relationship with his father.

Have you ever used prayer during tough negotiations?

Whether it's a negotiation, a difficult meeting, or a strained relationship, Martha and I will pause for a moment prior to facing the situation. We ask God, "Keep us in your will and keep our hearts going in the right direction. Keep us thinking about the best we can obtain for all in this meeting and help us to not become angry or self-serving. Keep our egos out of this, Father. Amen."

Here's an example. We had a meeting with a cast member and it was a difficult one, with many issues on both sides that hadn't been addressed. It had to be fixed, and quickly. Now, in the film business you don't go into one of these meetings and say, "Let's join hands and pray." Normally, people go in armed, angry, and defensive. We said a prayer beforehand, Martha and I asked the Lord to keep a guard at our mouths and to help us make the meeting respectful — to keep anger and suspicion from taking over. The meeting went very well.

We also spoke with Italian film producer Dino de Laurentiis, probably best known for his over-sized remake of *King Kong*.

He was constantly apologizing for his English, but I think what he had to say came across loud and clear.

Do you pray?

Talk about spirituality is not so easy. Spirituality is something inside of yourself. And we're jealous about what we have inside.

Jealous?

You know, my English is not too good. I hesitate to talk about my spirituality, because it is something that belongs only to me. And I do not think it's a good idea to put public what is my thinking, what is in my heart, what is in my soul in relation to God. Yes, I believe in God, but talk about the spirituality is not so easy.

Do you talk to God?

Well, even if I don't pray, I think about God. When I see every morning my little kids, there's God that keeps these kids well.

How many children do you have?

We have five children, the last two are seven and eight. Two little girls, the loves of my life. Every time I see my little girls in the morning, I think about God. This is the mys-

tery of life, the birth of a baby. This is the most beautiful mystery of life.

Any special words that you use?

I don't know if they are special. They come from my heart.

HOWARD SCHULTZ was working for a coffee company in Seattle and giving more than a passing thought to buying the business.

He spent hours poring over projected sales figures and researching every possible landmine that could explode if he decided to take that first step into uncharted territory. After scrutinizing the entire situation, Howard Schultz took the plunge.

Today he owns the titles of founder, chairman, and chief executive officer of Starbucks. It is quite a change from his years growing up in the federally subsidized projects of Brooklyn.

In the summer of 1987, prior to acquiring Starbucks, I prayed a great deal for the opportunity to be put in the position where my big dream could come true. It wasn't anything formal, but I found myself looking toward God for the wisdom to help me make it happen.

I know I found comfort in it, and also things did work out. I remember going back to a place, spiritually, where I said "thank you." I have tried to recognize the responsibility that I have. I think it goes deeper with me because I've tried to build the kind of company that my father never had a chance to work for.

So I prayed to God on an ongoing basis about this opportunity. I wanted to build a company that valued the human spirit, which did not leave people behind. That responsibility is not only about building profit, but about being the kind of person who does the right thing.

I remember praying that if I got this opportunity, if God would help me to make it happen, that I wouldn't abuse it. Today I thank God for the opportunity to have done just that.

Schultz plans to have more than two thousand Starbucks outlets in operation by, appropriately, the year 2000.

WE INTERVIEWED Ben Cohen and Jerry Greenfield about prayer. You probably know them as "Ben and Jerry."

They make ice cream — great ice cream, fantastic ice cream — the kind people with cholesterol problems should taste lightly of. Neither Ben nor Jerry prays in the conventional way.

Are you saying there was never a time in business when you said "God help me"?

BEN COHEN: The only time I ever said "So help me, God" was in court.

That's a good line.

JERRY GREENFIELD: I believe in a higher power or a greater intelligence or whatever you want to call it, but I don't find myself praying to that entity. I try to find myself getting into that natural law that governs us all.

What is that?

JERRY GREENFIELD: I was saying that to contrast the idea of praying. I think it's another way to be in touch with or fit in or be in harmony with this greater power.

BEN COHEN: Many times during the stress of our business we have been in tough spots and there appeared no rational way out of it, but we found it. I believe our lives are governed by spiritual laws and, in many respects, business is governed by spiritual laws. So just as individuals say it is better to give than to receive, I think when individuals get together to form a business, as this group gives, the business and the individuals will receive. That's a reason for success.

Now you need to do the business basics right, and there isn't much spirituality in that. You have to do the marketing plan right and the sales right and the finances. So, if you're doing the basics right while supporting the community, the community will support you back in the form of buying products. Infusing this spiritual dimension certainly helps.

I think the important thing is to take the things that we talk about in church or temple on Saturday or Sunday and bring them out into the real world — that's where most of our time is spent.

J. W. MARRIOTT is chairman and CEO of Marriott International. This hotel chain is rated one of the best one hundred companies to work for, according to *Fortune* magazine, and today they employ more than 225,000 people.

The company has come a long way since 1927, when Marriott's father, with five thousand dollars, opened a nine-stool root beer stand in Washington, D.C. Marriott International is now a twelve-billion-dollar company.

I have interviewed Marriott a number of times and attended numerous charity events at his many hotels throughout the United States. I reached him in between meetings — at, where else, a Marriott hotel — to talk about prayer.

I've always been taught it's not necessarily good to pray for the end result. But it's good to pray for assistance and help in whatever you need to do. There are lots of times during the day that I'll pray. And most of the time it's for a clear mind, good judgment, good sense, guidance, and direction. It isn't about should I own this hotel or just manage it.

I've come to believe that fasting is an important part of prayer. It cleanses the body and weakens you to the point where you are more humble and attuned with what you need to say, and it helps you listen.

When I fast and pray, I always say the prayer at the end. It's more effective in the end than it is in the beginning. I think you are more in tune with the spirit. It's hard for me to fast because my stomach gets messed up, but I find it to be helpful. Prayer is work and the Lord requires a lot of work sometimes.

Marriott, like my wife, Shawn, is Mormon. I have always made the point that both the Jews and the Mormons have a lot in common. After all, we were both wandering tribes in search of a permanent home. The Jews went east, the Mormons went west. We got the desert and they got Utah.

JUST AS we've become accustomed to seeing Starbucks and Marriotts, it is likely we're also used to seeing Blockbuster Video stores. Wayne Huzienga bought the company when it consisted of eight stores. He built it up to more than five thousand stores and sold Blockbuster to Viacom. It was a good business deal. He bought the company for thirty-two million dollars, and seven years later sold it for eight and one-half billion. Today he owns the Miami Dolphins and the Florida Marlins, the team that won the 1997 World Series.

I would say prayer is the most important thing that I do. When you're in prayer, you're not kidding anyone. You are saying exactly the way it is and that's the power of prayer. That alone requires faith and so the very act of prayer says you have faith. And if you didn't believe God was listening, you wouldn't pray.

I've never used prayer to make a deal. But I do use prayer in business a lot. There are times in business when things may not be going well, so I focus on being alone because it gives me a greater focus on the situation. But I am never really alone because I have God and that's the security that gives me the strength to go out and make things happen and accomplish my goals.

I don't recall sitting at my desk and saying, "Oh boy, help me get through this day." I guess maybe I haven't had any days that were that bad, you know? Sometimes we tend to think about praying in an emergency when something's gone wrong. But when you have the time to pray and you're there talking, it's just the two of you and that's a special time.

I've been so fortunate most of my life and I'd have to say most of my prayers have been answered. I sometimes wonder why. My wife and I talk about it a lot. It just keeps getting better and better.

> The things, good Lord, that we pray for, give us the grace to labor for.
> — SAINT THOMAS MORE

SUNSET BOULEVARD was a parking lot. The rabbi was at the wheel. We were at Sunset and

Robertson Boulevard, just east of Beverly Hills, and we'd moved only two blocks in ten minutes. I had to be at the Hollywood CNN studio in twenty minutes, and apparently so did everyone else in Los Angeles.

I was on the car phone to my producer, telling her I was on my way but the traffic was horrible. I used a few choice words to emphasize just how diabolical it was, and glanced over at Irwin. He seemed so calm and quiet and, damn it, at peace. "What is it?" I asked.

"Just saying a quick prayer for the book."

"You're driving in L.A. traffic. It's rush hour. We gotta be at the studio. And you're praying for the book? The book's got all the prayers it needs. What we need is lights, Irwin. Pray for green lights. Get us a straight shot down Sunset, and everybody in L.A. will buy a copy."

"I meant to ask, how did your conversations with the captains of industry go?"

"The suits in the big offices say they don't ask for things, only for strength and guidance. Personally, I'll bet there's a couple of them who pray for a good stock tip every now and then."

"Larry, there is nothing wrong with wealth. Enjoy it. But you must realize it is just one aspect of existence. If you were to have a face-to-face with God, what would you ask for? More wealth? Better health? Can I tell you a short story?"

"First, let me tell you one."

"Really?"

"Yep. It seems that Martin Buber, the philosopher, was having a discussion with a Catholic clergyman at a meeting at the Sorbonne in the 1920s. They were speaking about religious intolerance and the reasons for it.

"Buber said, 'Let me get this straight now. Except for the fact that you believe the Messiah has already come, and we believe the Messiah is yet to come, there really are no big differences in our faiths, correct?'

" 'You might say so,' responded the clergyman.

" 'But we can agree on the fact that the Messiah is not here now, so that being the case, let's get together and wait for the Messiah to come, and when he arrives we'll ask if he's been here before.' "

"A wonderful story, Larry, although theologically there are more significant differences between Judaism and Christianity than whether the Messiah has come yet or not."

"I'm sure, but you gotta admit, it's a good story, right?"

"It's a good story."

"Okay. Now yours." When you've got a good Martin Buber story, you can afford to be magnanimous.

"Okay. We tell this to school kids at Rosh Hashanah. A king punished his son by banishing him to a far-off province. The prince was coddled all his life, so he had no idea how to make a living. Finally, he decided to become a

215

shepherd. It was difficult, and the prince was exposed to the elements, but the labor required no special skills. He tried to build a hut from trees and branches to protect himself, like the other shepherds, but he just didn't have the skills to do it.

"After months and months of trying, the prince was greatly discouraged, to say nothing of being severely sunburned. Then he heard that the king would be visiting the nearby village. The custom was that anyone could write a request of the king on a piece of paper and try to throw it into the carriage as the king rode by. If the king read their request he would honor it.

"So the prince went to the parade and wrote on his piece of paper a request for a hut to shield him from the elements. He threw his request toward the king's carriage and, as luck would have it, the king opened it and read it.

"The king recognized his son's handwriting and began to weep. 'My child has forgotten that he is a prince. He does not ask to return to the palace where he can have everything. The greatest thing he can ask for is a hut to protect himself.' "

"Wait a minute!" I had to question this. "Wasn't the whole purpose of the banishment to teach the son humility? Now that his son has been humbled, the king is crying because his son isn't asking for more? What are we supposed to learn from this?"

"Larry, all of us are like the prince, and the

king is God. What are we going to ask God for? A bigger house? A better car? We have forgotten that we are princes and we can return to the palace. We can have anything we want, and we settle for a hut."

With that, the rabbi pulled in at the CNN studio. I looked at my watch and couldn't believe it — six minutes to spare.

"I'm early."

"Put the extra time to use and say thank you," the rabbi said.

"Thank you, Irwin."

"Not to me, Larry."

"Oh."

Chapter Eight
Prayer and Sports

Rabbi Katsof and I were sitting at Nate 'n Al's deli in Beverly Hills.

He was drinking Diet Snapple and watching me polish off a Bialystok roll. We were talking baseball. Correction, I was talking baseball, but the rabbi wasn't buying my theory about God being a Yankees fan. That was okay. I was used to the controversy.

I first formulated the theory while walking away from Ebbets Field that miserable autumn day in 1949 when God's team beat the Dodgers in the World Series. I was holding back tears, and Herbie Cohen said to me, "You know, Larry, there are some years when the Yankees lose too, so maybe it's not that God loves the Yanks. Maybe he just doesn't like the Dodgers." I responded in the same way Chicago Cubs have learned to answer such brutal observations. "Our day is coming," I told Herbie.

I had to wait six years until the Brooklyn Dodgers finally won a World Series over the hated Yanks; Red Smith or Jim Murray once said, "Rooting for the Yankees is like rooting for United States Steel." The series went seven games. Duke Snider hit four homers and the win was saved when Sandy Amoros made a fantastic catch in left field for the final out of the seventh inning — a sure hit by Yogi Berra who was usually a pull-hitter.

Luckily, the Dodgers' Walter Alston (was it God?) had replaced the other left fielder with Amoros, a left-handed player who wears the glove on his right hand. He was fast and reached out at the last minute with his right hand to make the catch. A right-handed outfielder would've had his glove on his left hand and could never have made that reach.

Whoever was ultimately responsible for that, it doesn't matter. What does matter is that Johnny Podres threw a 2–0 shutout that ended with a weak grounder from Elston Howard to Reese, and we were finally off the schneid. After what felt like two lifetimes, the Dodgers had won and millions of people cried with joy.

I was making my argument to Irwin about God being a Yankees fan, using the numbers. The Yankees won the World Series in 1927, 1928, 1932, 1936, and 1937. The Yankees, with God's help, took the 1941 series over my Brooklyn Dodgers, lost it to St. Louis the following year, and came back to win it from St. Louis in 1943. If you still need facts, the Yankees beat the Dodgers in a full set of games in 1947. You know what happened in 1949, and by 1956 God's team beat Brooklyn again. It was irrefutable.

"So how do you explain 1955?" the rabbi asked.

I was stumped. Where was my numbers man when I needed him? On my late-night radio show in the mid-1980s, I would get calls from this guy who lived in Paterson, New Jersey. He said he could predict the future based on the Mets' box score. He became a regular on the show and my audience started calling him "the numbers man."

The numbers man came up with some pretty elaborate statistical formulas which, if you followed his logic, were the bridge between the Mets' score and some topical event. Through the years the numbers man expanded his roster to include all the other Major League teams.

Here's an example of how the numbers man saw the world: He claimed the Yankees' 1984 season was stamped with the signature of God. On May 13, 1984, the Yankees won their thirteenth game. On June 13, 1984, the Yankees won their twenty-sixth game, and on July 13 the Yankees won their thirty-ninth game.

I trotted out the numbers man as my final proof that God was indeed a Yankees fan.

The rabbi said, "Well, Larry, the numerical coincidence is interesting, but I'm telling you God doesn't get involved in hockey."

Now, Nate 'n Al's is just about the loudest restaurant in Beverly Hills. But when I bellowed "Hockey?" at the top of my lungs, it was at the very moment that the place was quiet as everyone put more cream cheese on their poppy-seed bagels. My voice boomed out the door, down Beverly Drive, made a right at Wilshire, came up Rodeo Drive past all the up-scale shops, and took another left on Santa Monica Boulevard, knocking everyone off the sidewalk who happened to be in its path. It measured a 4.6 on the Richter scale and the Beverly Hills Police Department took fourteen calls within the next seven minutes about the earthquake.

Irwin was unfazed. "Hockey, volleyball, professional wrestling, it's all the same. I've heard boxers thank God for their right hook when they win and I can assure you God didn't have anything to do with their right hook or their victory, any more than God has anything to do with the Yankees."

"You're right," I said to the rabbi. "God wouldn't waste his time with a right hook. God's punch would be the uppercut — the first one thrown which ends the fight in the first round and has all the fans screaming for their money back."

The rabbi had that look in his eye.

"I know. I know what you're going to say, so don't say it," I said.

We both enjoyed the moment of silence. I thought back to an interview I had seen with Doris Kearns Goodwin when she was promoting her book about the Brooklyn Dodgers, called *Wait Until Next Year*. She talked about her prayer, as a Dodgers fan, that the Yankees would die in a train accident. I couldn't stand it any longer and I blurted out, "If he exists, I *just know* God helped Tommy Heinrich get that homer off Don Newcombe in 1949."

Forty-four percent of Americans believe prayer for victory in a sporting event is inappropriate.
— GALLUP SURVEY IN *LIFE* MAGAZINE
(DECEMBER 17, 1993)

ON SEPTEMBER 24, 1957, the Brooklyn Dodgers beat the Pittsburgh Pirates 3–0 in front of 6,702 people at Ebbets Field. It was the last game the Dodgers ever played as the baseball team from Brooklyn. In 1958, the Dodgers took the home field in Los Angeles and, wouldn't you know it, won the World Series the very next year.

Because everyone I know in Brooklyn holds grudges, we started rooting for any team the Dodgers played and continue to do so to this day. Interestingly enough, after forty years the Dodgers have been sold. To show Brooklyn's grudge can be placated, a committee of Big Apple politicians, steered by Brooklyn borough president Howard Golden, have worked to bring the team back where it belongs. What do you say, Mr. Murdoch?

Tommy Lasorda served as the Dodgers' manager, coach, player, and scout for forty-seven years, until he retired in 1996. However, just recently, he came out of retirement when Rupert Murdoch asked him to become the interim general manager of the Dodgers.

Besides being a decent fellow, Tommy was one heck of a manager. Before he was inducted into the Hall of Fame, he took the Dodgers to two World Series and four National League championships, while managing six All-Star teams. He's a close friend of mine and so, out of friendship, I've learned to temper my grudge against the Dodgers.

I keep a photo of Tommy on my desk. It's signed, "You and the Dodgers are great!" The man bleeds Dodger blue, and in his autobiography, *The Artful Dodger*, Lasorda took his passion to a higher level.

> **The Big Dodger in the Sky has seen fit to bestow upon me and mine a multitude of great moments during my years as leader of the pack.**
>
> — TOMMY LASORDA
> AND DAVID FISHER
> *THE ARTFUL DODGER*

I had his book in my hand while I was talking to him on the phone, and the voice I heard was different from the very vocal and excitable Tommy I thought I knew. We talked about how he attended Mass at his Catholic church every

Sunday during home games or, if on the road, at a local church. He spoke of the many times he invited ministers of all faiths to conduct prayer sessions in the Dodgers' clubhouse.

In all the years of doing schtick with Tommy Lasorda on a dais, and the laughs and the lengthy discussions about the designated-hitter rule, I hadn't seen this side of him. Before I could ask the first question, he was racing at top speed.

Nighttime is when conversation with the Big Dodger centers on his gratefulness for (1) his family, (2) the opportunities given him as a Dodger, and (3) his friends, coaches, trainers, and players. He never prays for himself, except to ask for the strength to do the right thing.

So, after a buildup like this, I had to ask if God makes the team win.

I think the Lord watches over us and inspires us and allows us to live the life he would want us to live. But I don't think he cares who wins the game. He doesn't get involved in things like that — that's up to the players and, I think, by having faith we can do our job better.

This is not to say that one of the most-winning managers in history hasn't asked for assistance during tight moments.

I remember the 1988 playoffs. I was in a situation where I only had one pitcher left, Orel Hershiser. The only other available pitcher, Jim Belcher, was back at the hotel and he was

scheduled to pitch the next day. I kept think-
ing to myself, "I'm putting my head in the
guillotine with Hershiser because he just
pitched eight and two-thirds innings the day
before. I brought him out of the bull pen with
two outs in the bottom of the twelfth inning
and the bases are loaded.

And when he walked out of the gate I prom-
ised God ten things real fast that I would do if
he got the out. He got it and no, Larry, I'm not
going to tell you the ten things, but I'd like to
hope God had a role in what happened that
day.

They must have been ten big things because
not only did the Dodgers win that game, but
they also won the World Series that year, beating Oakland four games to one.

IT IS standard practice before every baseball
game to play the national anthem. While the
crowd is on its feet singing, players stand with
their hats in hand, taking in the experience.

Some sing, some chew gum, and a few, like
Eric Davis of the Baltimore Orioles, pray. He's
been praying during the national anthem for
the past eighteen years, and jokes that he can
cover all the concerns between him and God,
depending upon who is singing.

Usually, if it's an a cappella group, one of the
members will try to hold a note longer than the
group before them and, by the end of the sea-

son, the national anthem can last five minutes — which is more than enough time for Number Twenty-four to talk to the Almighty.

I thank God for giving me the opportunity to go out on the field and allowing me to do the best that I can. Now, I'm aware that I'm praying and my teammates are praying, but the other team is praying too — so whose prayer gets answered?

Well, I think it's in the ability God gives you to do your own thing. You can pray to hit a home run, but if you don't swing the bat you won't hit a home run. He gives you the mentality and the ability to do it, but you still have to do it yourself. I think God is a neutral party in the game. He is everybody's fan.

Davis is quick to add that he prays off and on throughout the day. He told me he never allows prayer to occur at a particular time every day, other than before a ball game, because its practice should be spontaneous. It is something he does whenever he feels the need.

There's no particular time when I can say I prayed and it was answered. But there have been times in the outfield when I'll say, "Lord, don't let him hit this ball," and that's a prayer. And he might strike out. So, in a way, you don't think you are praying but that's exactly what you are doing. I mean, there have been times I've been sitting in the dugout with my teammates and I'll say something like "Oh Lord, I hope this man gets him out," or "Oh

*Lord, please don't allow him to hit this ball,"
and those are prayers.*

I have sat through games at Camden Yards in Baltimore when the score is tied, there are two outs, the bases are loaded, and we are into a Casey-at-the-bat situation. And during these exciting times I have looked about the stadium and seen people sitting quietly while everyone else is involved with "the wave" or shouting encouragement or, depending on their point of view, insults.

These people usually have their eyes closed and it is all too clear what they are doing.

I think it works. God's ears are being overloaded. You have a group of people praying for the same thing and it's coming in a hundred times stronger than if it's from just one person. God hears all the prayers, but if he keeps hearing this one prayer over and over again, well, of course it's going to matter. But God still makes the final decision on whether he'll answer the prayer or not.

Eric Davis underwent surgery for colon cancer in June of 1997 and was able to return to the Orioles three months later. He thinks the prayers of his family and friends had an effect during his operation and recovery.

I was given so many prayers from family and friends. I think we overloaded the Lord that day. They helped. Blessings can come in a number of ways. The Lord doesn't give you what you want, the Lord gives you what you need. For some reason you may not need to win that game. It might be a humbling experience, or a test of your character or a test of your faith.

Having the cancer removed from my body, well, my prayers were answered. I also prayed for us to win the World Series, but that didn't happen. I don't ask why. I just play with the cards I'm dealt and do it to the best of my ability.

Davis also told me that he thinks all prayers are answered, but many times they are answered in a way we weren't expecting or planning on.

I GUESS I had heard that phrase just about one time too many, because that leaves the playing field wide open for any answer. I can accept that God would send us a challenge so that we might learn from the experience, but we shouldn't need an Orphan Annie decoder ring to figure out the message he's trying to send.

So I put the question to the rabbi: If a prayer is answered, but we're not given the tools to decipher it and are not even aware it has been answered because so much mishagoss — Yiddish for "craziness" — has been piled on top of it, then the prayer really *hasn't* been answered. Or has it?

Another uncomfortable pause at the other end of the phone. Or maybe the discomfort was on my end? Let's see, if an uncomfortable pause occurs and there's nobody there to hear it . . .

"Larry, if a prayer is answered and your eyes aren't open, then of course you're not going to see it or understand it."

"Why can't God speak English? Why all the hoops?"

"What do you want? You want it delivered every morning like the newspaper? You want room service? You want a Larry Channel on your TV?"

I must admit, I started thinking about that last one and enjoying the idea. With all the TV shows I've done, they could program a Larry Channel twenty-four hours a day, seven days a week for several years without repeating a show. I had to get my mind off that prospect and back to the heat of debate.

"I want to understand it, Rabbi, that's all."

"You have to work at getting a conversation started, correct?"

"Correct."

"Can you have a conversation if one participant isn't listening?"

"No."

"Larry, God knows what we need. So we don't pray to God to remind him, we pray to God to remind ourselves. The essence of prayer is choice. Prayers help us refine and affirm what it is we want out of our lives. God desires our growth as human beings. Like any good parent, he doesn't spoil us by giving us what we want on a silver platter.

"We are confronted with obstacles, and we struggle when we lose awareness of God. Understanding isn't given, it is earned. We encounter roadblocks in life because we've lost sight of our path to God. Prayer is the map that leads us out of the wilderness and connects us to God."

"Hmm," I said, vamping for time and not really understanding.

"The concept of this is called 'the bread of shame.' Unless you earn it, you are spoiled. Let me ask you this: Were you an overnight success as a talk show host?"

"Hardly. I worked at it a long time, struggled for years."

"So it didn't come easy."

"No."

"Don't you think the struggle makes the success that much sweeter?"

I couldn't disagree. I looked out my hotel window and started thinking about something Lou Holtz said in our interview.

Faith is nothing more than believing when you have no proof. People say, "Show me proof and I'll believe." That's not faith. That's fact. There's a big difference.

— LOU HOLTZ

BRUCE JENNER is acknowledged to be one of the finest athletes to ever compete in the ultimate athletic challenge — the decathlon of the Olympic games. Consisting of ten track-and-field events in two days, the decathlon is a test not only of prowess and endurance, but will.

By the summer of 1976, Jenner had lost count of the hours invested in tuning his technique and timing. He was feeling the pressure of his own expectations of himself, and also from all the hoopla leading up to the competition.

Bruce Jenner knew he had to be in tune with himself to compete and there was only one way to do it. He prayed. But his prayers were tempered by an experience from the year before.

I had a friend who also ran the decathlon. He was a Christian, very religious, and he messed up one of the events. After it was over he came to me and said, "It was God's will." My first reaction to that was God wasn't the one who stepped out of the discus circle.

There's a fine point here, but you have to take responsibility for being able to use the power of prayer and take responsibility for your own life. I wouldn't have looked at it that way. I would have blamed it on me. If I foul three times, that's not God's fault. I'm the one throwing the discus.

Jenner spent the days prior to the competition having a conversation with God. He had never prayed regularly, except when major things happened in his life, and the 1976 Summer Games in Montreal were definitely in the category of major.

I was blessed with athletic gifts and being mentally able to handle high-pressure situations. I didn't want to waste those gifts, so I prayed for strength prior to the actual competition. It was, "Please get me through this." The Olympic games are the biggest pressure cooker in the world. You get one shot in front of the whole world — twelve years of preparation — and it is not, by any means, a fun day.

Leading up to it there is an enormous amount of fear, doubt, and pressure, and there are times when you really don't think you are going to survive the experience. So I prayed that I would be the very best I could possibly be under these pressures. I said, "Give me the power and then I'm outta here."

When Bruce Jenner left the field that day he was wearing a gold medal, having scored 8,364 points — which would remain the world record for five years and the American record for sixteen years. His picture was on every box of Wheaties, and all the newsmagazines and television shows carried stories about what he had accomplished in Montreal.

His life went into high gear and the speed at which things were being thrown at him was nothing for which he could have ever prepared. A few days later, when Jenner had another conversation with God, it was simply a thank-you for getting him through the event.

Today, Jenner is happily married, living in California, and the father of ten children. Though not competing anymore, he travels the country talking about the lessons the Olympics experience taught him.

Bruce Jenner has had some time to reflect on the relationship between prayer and sports.

It's a game. It's not life-and-death, but it reflects a lot on life and the individual. The ability to overcome tremendous obstacles in your life is just a part of it. It takes a lot to compete in sports and do well. God doesn't look over the game and God doesn't care who wins or loses. But I do think he cares about the souls that are out there and the impact this game will have on their life, for good or for bad.

Some people handle it better than others — the fame, the money, the demands for time. The big picture is where is God leading the athletes? That is more important than the game. It's more important than anything inside the twenty-yard line. God is interested in how this will affect them the rest of their lives.

It teaches them about winning and losing and how to handle success and how to get ahead in life, because nobody gives anything away in sports. They have to work for it. And those are lessons to be learned in life.

OUR JOURNEY through sports and prayer had to take us to Notre Dame, which is said to be God's alma mater. Personally, I think the reason Notre Dame consistently came out ahead in the box score was that coach Lou Holtz was on the sidelines. Holtz coached the Fighting Irish for eleven seasons and a hundred victories, and he's the first to say that God was the twelfth player on the field for Notre Dame.

I didn't pray to win, but I prayed to do everything to glorify God by my actions, although I didn't always accomplish that. We said the Hail Mary before a game and we always went to a team Mass before we went to the stadium. The priest gave the homily — we'd do this on the road as well as at home.

If a team member was not Catholic they didn't have to participate in the Mass, but they had to attend. I never had any player say, "I don't want to be a part of this." We covered it in recruiting by saying this is part of Notre Dame.

The Coach — Lou Holtz is always The Coach, even when he isn't a coach — told us that whether he is on the field during a game or engaged in some other activity, his conversations with God, though brief, are effective.

You pray during the game but you don't get down on your knees. I'm praying to establish a relationship with God, and then I think you move on with your life and try to do something the way God would like for you to do it. I say something like, "God help me to think clearly here," and, boom, you move on. That would be a typical prayer during a game — "Help me to be clear and help me evaluate the situation."

I like to think that most of the praying was done beforehand, but in the game plan I always had five different sayings written down. You know, "Ask and you shall receive, seek and you shall find, knock and it shall be open to you." I also include Proverbs 3:5, which says, "Trust in the Lord with all your heart and lean not unto thine own under-standing." Just positive passages.

You gotta remember, I'm busy making decisions and I've been doing this for years. So I break the field down by area and there's room for five sayings. And no, I'm not going to give you all five, so don't waste my time asking.

I didn't ask but I did the math — a prayer for every twenty yards. Who am I to argue if that's the right ratio, especially against someone who has won as many big games as The Coach? I found myself wishing I'd known about this when I was betting more money than I could afford to lose on horses that always seemed to run out of gas in the last quarter-mile at race-tracks around America.

I asked The Coach's impression of a player dropping to one knee after scoring a touch-down.

I think if it's sincere that's fine, but if he then goes out and gets arrested for abusing a girl, well, then you have to think.

Did you pray after every win?

I prayed after every game. We usually said a Hail Mary and on certain occasions I would lead the team in a prayer. You had to be careful in certain schools because of the American Civil Liberties Union, but at Notre Dame you didn't have to worry and that was a real blessing.

We prayed before every meeting and we probably had one hundred meetings a year — team meetings. We grabbed hands, bowed our heads, and prayed in silence. Everybody prayed in their own way, but we always prayed for one another.

If you lost the game was the prayer different?

No. You pray to lead your life the right way and to handle whatever comes along. If you win, you want to be humble. If you lose, you want to be gracious and make your resolve even greater.

Holtz says he knows Notre Dame fans in the stands say prayers in tight situations and he is convinced this unofficial group prayer is effective. The proof might be found in his winning record but he cites the Bible, which says if two or more pray together, the Lord will be in your presence. Saturday afternoons at Notre Dame bring eighty thousand people to the stadium. Now that's presence.

> For when the One Great Scorer comes to write against your name, he marks not that you won or lost, but how you played the game.
>
> — GRANTLAND RICE
> LEGENDARY SPORTS EDITOR,
> *NEW YORK HERALD TRIBUNE*

STEVE YOUNG, All-Pro quarterback for the San Francisco Forty-Niners, is a devout Mormon and one of the most prolific passers in the history of the National Football League. We asked him about his prayers, his faith, and football.

First of all, prayer is a literal communication with God. It's an opportunity, a gift the Lord has given us – a constant chance to communicate. I don't pray to win because that's not appropriate. I pray for safety and for clarity of mind. There have been many times when I have left the sidelines for the field and I say a quick prayer for clarity of mind. That's the most important and that's the greatest gift that I could get.

So much of my game is utter reaction. There is no pre-thought, so the clearer and more precise your mind is, the more effective you'll be in the job. My job is all about subconscious reaction.

A pass is in the air — do you pray that Jerry Rice will catch it?

No, I hope that he catches it. I don't think

the Lord is that interested. That's not a prayer. That's a hope. Maybe it's different, and this isn't to say the Lord isn't interested in football, because he is in terms of the people and their needs and their righteous desires. The Lord is paying attention on game days. The Lord cares for everybody. But I think a lot of the Lord's purposes are served by losing as much as by winning.

How about when the Forty-Niners are kicking a field goal and are down by two points?

I hope for a field goal. I say something, but I don't say it to the Lord. But there have been times when I've been downtrodden emotionally or physically with football, and I'm down to my wits' end, and the kicker goes out there and I think to myself, "Oh Lord, please, just this one time, make it go through."

But my greatest learning moments from heaven have been when it didn't go through. Early in my career I was struggling to make a name for myself behind Joe Montana and there was pressure to perform, and I think if everything had gone smoothly I would never have become the man I am now.

So many times we learn by unanswered prayers. So many times there are prayers we say — "Gee, if this would just work out once" — but what we need isn't always what we want, it's what the Lord knows is best for us. The purpose of mortality is to learn.

Can you tell me how you pray?

I open with the words "My Heavenly Father" and then I try to set my mind to things I am grateful for and let him know how much I appreciate them. And then I let my mind go to what I feel my needs are and what I need help with, and then I go to places where I ask for blessings on my family or someone who is struggling.

Many times I've fallen asleep on my knees at my bedside and wakened kneeling. I've had to say, "I dozed off, Lord, and I don't know where I left off, but you know what I'm saying." I close every prayer in the name of Jesus Christ.

How would you explain prayer to someone who hasn't done it?

I think the first thing you have to understand is that it is truly an act of faith. To me, the first principle of the Gospel is faith and faith is misunderstood because it is something that isn't seen.

For someone who goes by just what they see, faith can be an uncomfortable feeling. Someone who wants to pray has to give that feeling of faith a shot — that feeling that I don't know for sure and I don't know what the difference is, but I'm just going to kneel and pray. That's essential. Faith is a muscle that you have to exercise. The more you do it, then the more the spirit will be able to affect your life. You get stronger and more spiritually-minded.

Do you pray after the game?

Yeah, as I've gotten older — and I'll be sitting in front of my locker dead tired — my perspective has broadened. Those are special moments at the end when the pressure is off and there's a sense of accomplishment. I'm stripped down to my shorts, I'm tired and beat up, and it's just "Lord, I'm so grateful for this moment." I find myself saying that more now than when I was younger.

Time and experience in life brings wisdom and that's why older people are smarter than younger people. When I was eighteen I thought I knew everything, but I didn't know anything. And I know I'll look back and say, wow, when I was thirty-five I thought I knew everything, but I still knew very little.

How about the prayers of fans?

I look at them as support. I don't believe the Lord is involved in picking winners. The Lord teaches just as much when the ball goes outside the goal, but I feel the fans' desires. I know fans who watch only in certain shirts or watch only when we have or don't have the ball, and it's a way to bring good vibes and karma, but I'm not sure that's a prayer. It's a hope.

MARK DISMORE has raced in the Indianapolis 500 three times — 1991, 1996, and 1998. But it's his first race that people talk about because during a qualifying run Dismore was coming into turn four — at 210 miles per hour in his four-year-old Penske car with a Buick engine — when he hit the wall.

It was Friday, May 10, and it happened at 5:10 P.M. [Two five-tens — call the numbers man.] We were running real good, probably good enough for the twelfth position. I was trying to go faster because I wanted to get everybody's attention — to get a good job driving race cars for a living.

Coming out of turn four I brushed the wall, and it wasn't a big deal because I remember thinking to myself, "I'll just slow down." Well, the right-rear wheel cantered out and the car spun. In a flash I realized I was going backwards and I said out loud, "Oh, my God." I remember that as clear as I'm talking to you now. I slid into the inside wall and ricocheted off and hit square into the pit wall. The car exploded and the total distance traveled in the wreck was a quarter-mile.

The car broke up, the motor broke off the back, the front end was torn off the car. I came to rest with my legs on the ground. There wasn't any car remaining. I was conscious and remember thinking, "Thank God, I'm alive," and then I said, "I can't believe I'm alive." I thanked God right there.

Now I don't pray before the race. I feel like God has a lot better things to do than worry about race-car drivers. But in that car, I was saying a prayer. I had a broken neck and a broken wrist, my knees were broken and my ankle was broken and, most of all, my heart was broken. I wanted to be a race-car driver at Indy. I prayed for the strength to get better.

They took me to an infield hospital and my wife, Donna, came to see me — she sits in the stands and prays around every turn in every race. I was put in a helicopter and taken to Methodist Hospital where they were able to put Humpty Dumpty back together again. I prayed to lead a normal life and be able to take walks with my wife and kids.

I think prayer is putting your faith in something you can't see or understand. We have to learn there are lots of things not in a human being's control. You have to just say there is a greater power than man.

Mark Dismore was back in a race car in late December of that year, testing a Dan Gurney Toyota. He is now driving cars for Kelly Racing and, like many other Indianapolis 500 drivers, he thinks turn four has an unsettling personality. For whatever reason, it is that turn where most of the wrecks occur at this famous track. Mark Dismore says he includes turn four in his prayers now.

WE TOOK the issue of prayer and sports to Kareem Abdul-Jabbar who knows something about both topics. He turned to Islam in the early 1970s while playing center for the Milwaukee Bucks. In college he led the UCLA Bruins to three consecutive NCAA championship titles — a feat which has never been repeated.

By the time he retired from the NBA in 1989, after playing for both the Bucks and the Lakers, Kareem had been named to the NBA All-Star Team eighteen times, had been on six championship teams, was named Most Valuable Player six times, and became one of the highest scorers in NBA history, racking up 38,387 points. And if that isn't enough, he retired holding nine NBA records, some of which still stand to this day.

How do you think prayer works?

It helps you understand that there is a bigger plan to everything. It makes you humble. I refer to our Scripture, knowing that the Koran contains the plan for mankind and what happens on earth. That's something we all must submit to. Islam means submission.

When you realize that, it humbles you with regard to your own personal agenda. You have to see the selfishness, for many people think that the divine will and their will are identical. We have that type of vanity — we have to get over it. I think prayer helps with that.

What works and what doesn't work?

Following the divine path is what works. Mankind always tries to strike out on its own path at times.

A person who doesn't know this — do you think they can still connect with God?

Everything that you learn about in religion has to do with right and wrong. Everything up to the point of action is theory. When you get to the point of action, that's where real righteousness is defined. Anybody can do a righteous act, it doesn't have to be someone who has my religious background or any particular religious background. Right and wrong is usually obvious.

What do you get out of prayer?

Prayer is just discipline for me. I see it as something the Supreme Being gave us to refer us continually back to the plan. It helps to straighten our path.

Do you feel good after prayer?

Yes. It's a moral obligation and it does put good on your scale. Our concept of how we'll be judged is more or less the same as in Judaic Law. We will be judged on the balance, our good deeds — we want that side of the scale heavy.

Did you ever pray when you were playing basketball?

No, that's vanity. That's a temporal goal. If I played football, I'd probably pray more, because there's a certain amount of pain with that game, and injuries. It's going to happen to everyone — they know it. It's like every time they go out there they're rolling the dice. They're very fortunate to make it through the game without a serious injury.

Is God a Lakers fan or a Yankees fan?

I don't think so. Certainly not a Yankees fan.

You've been very successful, very blessed in many areas of your life. Do you feel your relationship with God had anything to do with this?

I think the moral anchor that Islam gave me enabled me to withstand the temptations that knocked a whole lot of people out of the saddle. A lot of people get out of whack when they're given a whole lot of money and attention and told that they're wonderful. They decide that they are, and then start doing some really bad things. You need a moral anchor. My faith has given me that.

Do you feel an obligation to God?

To try and live a moral life. Always encourage good and condemn evil in whatever ways that you can — that is an obligation on all of us. Someone like myself, in the public eye, probably has more of an obligation. That's how I see it. I'm not saying everyone's supposed to see it that way, but that's how I see it.

For readers who may be interested in connecting to God, what advice would you give them?

I would tell them to know themselves. You can't know anything beyond yourself until you know yourself. Where you begin and end — that's the whole concept. You have to understand that.

What's our role in the universe?

The Supreme Being gave Adam the planet and told him to take care of it. Until something else is divined, I think we're supposed to take care of that, and deal with each other and increase our knowledge. The prophet Muhammad said to seek knowledge from the cradle to the grave, even if you must travel as far as China — that was the furthest place from Arabia that they knew. We have been exhorted to go to great lengths to accumulate knowledge.

OF ALL the powerful people I've met, no one has more charisma than Muhammad Ali. I have been at banquets, sports awards shows, and charity events, and when Ali walks in, the room changes. He has a magnetism.

Ali won three heavyweight titles during his professional boxing career. His fights also included a battle with the United States over his status as a conscientious objector during the Vietnam War — a fight he eventually won in a unanimous Supreme Court decision four years later, but not before being banned from boxing and stripped of his WBA and WBC heavyweight titles.

I visited Muhammad Ali on a rainy spring afternoon at his Berrien Springs, Michigan, home. We sat for an hour talking about prayer

— in between demonstrations of Ali levitating his body off the ground (I still don't know how he does it) and Ali's-Hidden-Handkerchief-in-the-Hand trick (I got that one). Parkinson's disease may have lowered the volume on Ali's banter, but the spirit which drives his wit remains.

He is Muslim and prays five times a day, facing Mecca. On the back of a chair by the fireplace is a neatly folded prayer rug upon which he kneels when connecting with Allah.

It's February 25, 1964. You're in Miami and you are about to face Sonny Liston in the ring. Were you praying before you stepped in?

Yes.

What were you praying for?

I prayed to win. I did that before all my fights. I prayed to win. And I prayed that I wouldn't lose.

You won in seven rounds.

[Ali smiles]

Did you say prayers while running in Pennsylvania during training?

No. I don't pray when I'm running. And I don't pray when I'm boxing. I've already done that when I'm in the ring.

April 25, 1967. You refused induction into the armed services because you were a conscientious objector to the Vietnam War. Tell me about your prayers that day.

I don't pray for vanity. I said no more prayers during Vietnam than at any other time. I did pray though, and what I said was between Allah and me, so I'm not going to tell you about it.

Do you think your prayers to Allah are heard more than another's prayers to Allah?

I would never think that.

In the few fights you lost — Ken Norton, Joe Frazier — what did you pray after the contest?

Well, I didn't ask what happened. I never asked why I didn't win. I was grateful to finish. I always said, if I lose, it could be worse. I never asked for Allah's protection from these fighters.

When do you pray?

I pray before every airplane I'm on takes off. Planes crash. I pray before every meal I eat. But when I miss one of the five prayers [he points to his heart] I'm unhappy.

You can feel it?

I can feel it. That's right.

Did you pray earlier this year when there was a possibility we could go to war with Iraq?

I prayed it wouldn't happen. It didn't.

Was that the result of your prayer?

[Ali smiles]

What advice would you offer me about prayer?

I wouldn't. If you don't care, then it's not important to you.

We have really learned how to pray

when we realize that prayer is a privilege
rather than a duty.

— ANONYMOUS

RABBI KATSOF and I were in Mendy's, the only
kosher sports bar known to mankind. Irwin said
he had to talk to me urgently, and I had to watch
a football game.

Some people relax on Sunday with a book,
some people go to a museum, the rest of us
watch football. I had wagered fifty dollars on
the New York Jets in a football game in December. The odds were against me 'cause I can't
remember the last time the Jets won a meaningful game in December, but Parcells was coach-
ing them now and I was feeling optimistic.

"All right, Irwin, it's half-time. Talk to me
now or forever hold your peace."

"I have been thinking about how I can move
you off the fence."

"Yeah?"

"Then it dawned on me — you're a betting
man. You like to gamble."

"Right."

"Ever gamble on a long shot?"

"I have the Jets, don't I? Be hard to find a
longer shot than the Jets in December."

"So what do the odds have to be before you'll
take a chance on God? Ten percent? Fifteen
percent? A wise teacher once told me, 'Find
out what you're prepared to die for, and then

don't die for it — live for it."

"Ten percent isn't much of chance, Rabbi."

"Have you ever bought a lottery ticket?"

I was silent.

"I rest my case," the rabbi said. The game was about to start back up, so the rabbi said his goodbyes and told me God would send me understanding if I just kept asking questions.

I sat there thinking about what Coach Holtz had said about faith and proof. All my life I've survived on street smarts, but never did very well in school. And now I had something right in front of me, prayer, that requires no intellectual or academic credentials — an arrangement I would certainly welcome at any other time, but I'm unhappy. Why?

If only God wasn't a Yankees fan.

Chapter Nine
Prayer and Politics

In our home there was always prayer — aloud, proud, and unapologetic.
— *PRESIDENT LYNDON JOHNSON*
WASHINGTON PRAYER BEAKFAST (1964)

Ralph Reed has been on the front lines of the growing influence of religion in American politics.

Until September of 1997, Ralph headed the Christian Coalition, a much admired or much maligned — depending on your point of view — organization that has probably done more to elect Republican majorities in the House and Senate than any other political action group.

Through local grass roots organizations, bulk mailings, and massive voter-guide distribution, the Christian Coalition has flexed its political muscle at the ballot box. Ralph Reed recently stepped down as head of the Christian Coalition, but has moved even deeper into the political arena with the opening of his political consulting office, Century Strategies.

Have you ever prayed for legislation on the Hill?

I don't pray for the victory of a particular candidate or the passage of a particular bill. I tend to view such prayers as carnal and temporal in nature. I do pray that the Lord's will be done through the process and that he will, ultimately, be glorified. I think sometimes God can be glorified in defeat.

Give us an example.

I certainly think when Abraham Lincoln lost in 1858, it didn't mean the end of the anti-slavery cause. Two years later he was president. I don't think you can view defeat in human terms.

Instead, you have to see defeat as preparation for ultimate victory. The most important prayer for a politician is the prayer Christ taught his disciples — "Thy Will Be Done." Your focus should not be on winning the immediate victory, your focus should be on God's will. Sometimes, in the providential world of God, the good guys lose a few.

Why do the good guys lose a few?

We don't always understand it, but we know it happens. We know God allows it to happen.

So when a candidate you back wins, do you read this as your prayers being answered or God's will being done?

I don't get that spiritual about it. Obviously I'm happy, but I focus more on the responsibility that comes from victory.

Do you think on election night that God is paying attention to what is going on?

Yes, I think God cares about the affairs of men and women. I think he cares about the heads of nations and leaders. I don't think it's the most important thing, but God cares whether we have good leadership or not.

Is a president's prayer heard more than someone else's prayer?

Some people have a title and other people have a testimony. Pharaoh had a title. Moses had a testimony. Herod had a title. John the Baptist had a testimony. Joseph was in prison, but he had a powerful testimony. God heard his prayer and acted upon it. I think the focus is on the character and the testimony of the one praying. It's not on the temporal offices that they hold.

If a piece of legislation that you support gets defeated, is that something God has done?

No. I see that as something he has allowed, in his providential plan, to happen.

Is it a lesson?

I think you can be made stronger by defeat or more seasoned or wiser or humbled and chastened and, maybe, more dependent on God than on your own ability. When Martin Luther King Jr. was unable to break a filibuster in the Senate with the March on Washington in 1963, I don't think that meant God intended for African Americans not to treated the same under the law as whit

I think what it meant was God want it in a particular way that was diff the way Martin Luther King Jr. wanted to do it. And it turned out God's plan was greater, because if we go back and look at the old black-and-white footage of the March on Washington, what we remember is the I Have a Dream speech and the prophetic nature of that moment. We don't remember that the march was a political failure.

But, in the grand panorama of God's plan for humanity, it was a success because it was a voice of moral resonance speaking with tremendous prophetic power at a time of immense pain. When you are attempting to be a person of faith in a political system, your focus has to be lifting up a banner of justice to which the faithful will rally. . . . You don't focus on winning an election or defeating a bill.

Do you think the prayers of the Christian Coalition have made America a better place?

I don't want to particularize it to the Christian Coalition. I think there are millions of devout and faithful people who have prayed for this nation. I believe prayer is effective. It makes a difference. One of the things the Bible teaches us to do is pray for our leaders. It doesn't say pray for leaders of the political party with which you are affiliated. It doesn't say pray for Ronald Reagan but not Bill Clinton. That's something we have to rediscover.

Do you include Bill Clinton in your prayers?

Yes. I pray for our national leaders, that

254

they will be wise and that they will be fair and judicious. I hope that liberals said the same prayer when Ronald Reagan was in the White House. On the day Reagan was shot, I think every American prayed for his health and his protection. Maybe there were some who didn't, but I think most did.

I PUT the question of politics and prayer to Jerry Falwell, who ran the politically active Moral Majority from 1979 until 1989.

At its peak, it raised more than eleven million dollars in one year to keep an eye on the White House, Congress, and the Supreme Court.

Falwell says there is not only a place for prayer in the political arena, but a need.

Look at First Timothy, chapter two, which says we are to pray for those who are in authority. We are to pray for the king, and in our case that's the president. So I pray that God gives them wisdom and protects them. I don't think there is any difference between sacred and secular for a believer. God is interested in every area of our lives. He wants us to win and often we win when we lose, which is one of the best lessons to learn.

I believe in human responsibility. So I look at candidates who best represent what I believe and who will do best for most people and who I think know best for the country, and I work very hard to get them in office. But then, after having done my best, I leave it in the hands of God. It is the will of God after I do my best.

POLITICAL COLUMNIST and Fox Television pundit Cal Thomas says there is a place for prayer in politics, but he has words of caution for those who think the ballot box is the way to convert the country.

I have prayed with Jimmy Carter. I went to Sunday school with him to see the dynamics of his classes and I prayed for him as president. I pray for Bill Clinton. And now that I think about it, I don't think I pray for Bill Clinton enough.

But I have prayed to God to let this or that conservative win an election. God puts people in authority he wants to watch over us. So it wasn't an accident Clinton was elected again. I think it was a tweak at the Christian Coalition and the other groups who thought they were going to usher in legislation on the backs of the political leaders. I hope it was a lesson to them. The kingdom of God isn't going to arrive on Air Force One, *no matter who's on the plane.*

Although he's regularly asked to do so, God does not take sides in politics.
— SENATOR GEORGE MITCHELL
CONGRESSIONAL HEARING, JULY 13, 1987

I WAS waiting for a flight at Washington's Dulles airport and decided to call Irwin on the issue of prayer and politicians.

"Rabbi, we have all these folks saying God wants us to pray for our leaders. Now, if you have all these people praying for one guy, sort of like having all the Notre Dame fans praying for Notre Dame, then God's gonna hear those prayers, right?"

"God will get involved in the matter of sports and politics only insofar as it impacts the human relationship to truth. The Almighty has one goal — mankind's ultimate pleasure — but he cannot live man's life."

"But if God hears all these prayers for one guy, say everyone praying for Bill Clinton, well God's gonna do something, right?"

"Maybe, maybe not. God may not do what you think he should do," was the rabbi's answer.

"Irwin, if God is going to do whatever God wants to do, then why should I waste my time praying in the first place? On one hand, you say God is all-powerful, but then you tell me I have free will. You say to ask and I shall receive, but it may not be what I expected or wanted. I can't keep up with this. The ground keeps shifting under my feet."

"Larry, let me give you a parable about man's relationship to God."

"A parable? That's another word for one of your short stories?" I was needling him, but the truth is that I was beginning to look forward to his tales.

"When a parent teaches a child to walk, he encourages the child to take two or three steps toward him. As the child moves closer, the parent backs away. He doesn't do this out of meanness, but to encourage the child to walk more. In the same way, God will sometimes appear to withdraw from our lives. We should not take this as a sign of displeasure or rejection. God is withdrawing to arouse us to intensify our search for him."

"Rabbi, let's cut to the chase. Can you pray to defeat a political opponent?"

"You can pray for results, but there has to be more to it. Do you want to win so you can improve the quality of life, or do you want the power of the office? Do you want the prestige of being a congressman or do you want to represent the welfare of the people? Prayer reveals a lot about the person who is praying."

I'm not one to pray for senators, but when I look around and see them I find myself saying a prayer for our country.
— ED HALE, U.S. SENATE CHAPLAIN

JOHN MCCAIN may have lost the battle, but he hasn't given up the war. He spent most of 1997 trying to get the votes in place for the campaign finance reform bill which became known as

McCain-Feingold — named for Senator John McCain, a Republican from Arizona, and Senator Russell Feingold, a Democrat from Wisconsin — and was defeated in the 105th Congress.

Had it been successful, soft money would not have been able to find its way into a political campaign and, as a result, financial support could be more easily tracked. McCain told me he will try again in the 106th Congress.

And if he is successful, prayer will have had nothing to do with it.

I don't pray for legislation. I pray that I will be given the wisdom to do the right thing and the tenacity to see it through like I'm doing right now with campaign finance reform. In Congress I'm praying all the time, but it is for the right thing and to have the strength to keep doing it, if indeed it is the right thing.

Now, I think God is all-knowing but I don't think God dictates what our political fortunes are going to be or what they should be. We do that. And that's how you can accept things like Bosnia or the Holocaust. That's the misdeeds of man.

But there are times when I'm rising in the Senate elevator and I'll just close my eyes and say a prayer for strength. Sometimes I pray when I'm driving. There is always time to pray, even for a senator. So I don't pray for success of a bill or for failure of a bill I'm opposed to. I pray to be able to do right.

CHRISTOPHER DODD, first elected to the Senate in 1980, is now serving his third term representing the people of Connecticut.

He has the distinction of being the youngest person in Connecticut elected to the Senate and the first Connecticut son to follow his father to the upper chamber of Congress. Christopher Dodd was general chairman of the Democratic Party and is very active in legislation that affects American families.

Is there any legislation that comes to mind for which you have used prayer?

Let me share some generic thoughts. I think most people in public life treat prayer as a private matter. Maybe it's generational, maybe it's how we were raised.

There have been occasions through the years when I didn't think there was much hope of getting certain members to support a bill that I thought had a lot of merit and value. I asked, in quiet moments, for an intercession that certain members might see the benefit the bill would bring to people.

I've only asked for divine intercession on a few occasions, but I did ask for it on the Family and Medical Leave Act when I saw parents at the National Institutes of Health or at a Ronald McDonald House who were spending time with their children far away from their homes. The parents were anxious over whether or not they were going to lose their jobs because they had taken all their available time to be with their sick child.

The Family and Medical Leave Act allowed parents twelve weeks of unpaid leave. In that case I prayed for God to intercede because that was something which affected people's lives tremendously.

You used prayer because it was that close?

The bill was vetoed twice. I won one veto override. I was hoping and praying that President Bush would see the light. Later, Jim Baker told me they should have never vetoed the bill and he doesn't know how it happened. When I needed to override the veto in the Senate, I received support from people I didn't think I was going to have. We overrode that veto. Not in the House, I didn't ask the Lord for the House. I made a mistake — I should have made it a broader question.

The Family Medical Leave Act was signed in January of 1993.

Yes, President Clinton campaigned for it. After his election, I had to get a simple majority for passage. Previously, I had to get sixty-seven votes. It was only the second veto President Bush had overridden in the Senate. That was one moment when I used prayer.

How about during an election?

You should be judicious when you ask for the Lord's intercession. I ask the Lord to help me do the right thing but I don't ask him for votes. I think when you get to questions of spirituality, prayers are for love, for a sense of

261

forgiveness, for understanding, wisdom, strength — which is what I prayed for in the Family and Medical Leave Act. Those are the things for which I ask the Lord's intercession.

The good Lord isn't constrained by the human frailties of impatience, so you shouldn't feel restrained in how often you ask him for help. However, I try to be a little more patient knowing the Lord gets many requests.

Was your prayer during the enactment of Family and Medical Leave for certain members to vote the way you wanted them to?

I didn't focus on individuals. There were people I hoped we could convince of the wisdom of the idea because it could make a difference in people's lives. Dr. Koop [former U.S. surgeon general] will tell you the best thing for a sick child is a familiar face.

Did you win because of prayer?

Well, I certainly think it had a huge influence. I remember being very surprised at some of the votes I got, and I had no indication before the vote that I would receive them.

Want to name names?

No, I don't.

Family Leave was vetoed twice. Why do you think God made you work so hard?

Well, I think it became a better bill. There's a reason we go through this process. We like to think our first draft is the best, but as Hemingway said, "Brilliance emerges in the eleventh draft." We had to compromise and I think the ultimate bill was better.

What about the Persian Gulf War? Did you pray when the president told you we were going to go?

The hardest vote I ever cast is the vote that will place another in harm's way. I've never been asked to vote on a declaration of war, but that would be the hardest one to cast. Clearly, when events like the Gulf War are going to happen, you pray for the safety of those involved. As I believe in the existence of the Lord, I believe in the existence of evil. And every now and then it manifests itself in an incarnate way.

DURING ORRIN HATCH's first term as a Republican senator from Utah, Democrats were in the majority and there was movement within the Senate to replace the Electoral College — our system of electing a president — with a popular vote. Hatch was against it for fear that the most populous states would receive all the attention from candidates and Utah, which has only two million people, would be ignored.

The day of the vote I was alone in my Senate office and I said a prayer. I was on my knees. I asked for help throughout the process and I asked for help in getting enough senators to see it our way.

Then I went to the Senate floor and one of the members of the opposite side came up to

263

me and said, "Orrin, you are going to win this today." He was in shock. We not only won, we won going away. It was a very important vote.

In another case, I was the only Republican who was for the Childcare Development Block Grant. I convinced the Democrats to change the bill, from a big federal bureaucratic bill, to block grants to the states. President Reagan was against it, Senator Dole was against it, and most Republicans were mad about it.

When the final vote came to the floor, Bob Dole came to me and asked for a voice vote, because he knew we were going to win big. We passed the Childcare Development Block Grant unanimously in the Senate and then it passed the House, and it is now helping millions of children all over this country.

I know that there was extra help in each of these cases. I think marvelous things come through prayer. I think that we can be inspired in everything we do in our daily lives if we just live righteously and worthy of God's blessings. I've been inspired by people who put their lives into God's hands, who got on their knees, humbled themselves and prayed, who really tried to do God's will.

It doesn't mean we won't go through trials and tribulations. That's the way we're refined – that's the way we are made into great people.

Senator Hatch says he never bargained with God, but he admits having mentioned in his prayers just how devoted he is.

I have never made but one prayer to God, a very short one: Oh God, make my enemies ridiculous.

— VOLTAIRE

POLITICS IS often said to be war without weapons. Jeane Kirkpatrick was United States ambassador to the United Nations for four years of the Reagan administration, and in that position endured confrontations with her counterparts from other countries over myriad issues. It was during this time that she found herself praying for help through the conflict.

It was a very difficult job and I started to pray fairly regularly during those years at the UN. The United Nations was a mentally overwhelming experience, with so much discord and hate, so many lies. It was very hard to bear. They were the Cold War years and they were also years of greater than usual violence in the Middle East. So, mainly, I prayed for wisdom and forbearance.

There were times I felt I couldn't continue to listen to the quality of the debate and attacks and lies that went on in the Security Council. I prayed for personal composure because there were attacks on the United States that just went for hours and hours on end. There were attacks on Israel too, and I prayed that God might help them overcome their hate for Israel. I kept my composure, but I don't think anyone who hated Israel overcame their hatred.

WE TALKED with Alexander Haig, President Nixon's chief of staff during Watergate. The threat of impeachment was in the air then too. We asked if he ever said any prayers.

I couldn't afford to draw conclusions that things were going badly because I wanted to do everything I could to make the president succeed, and yet I could see it was going to be a very hard thing to do. It was a political struggle that took it outside the span of spirituality. It was who would have the power — those who didn't like Nixon or those who supported Nixon?

I prayed many, many, many times. And those prayers weren't for some kind of answer about whether the president was going to survive or whether we should or shouldn't make a deal but, instead, I kept asking for guidance. I was in the midst of having to make instantaneous decisions and, as a result, there was no time whatsoever to reflect. You just had to do it.

So when you had a spare moment you prayed that whatever it was that was sustaining you would keep you from doing something stupid or wrong. Those were quiet and private prayers in the White House.

I've been driven to my knees because I know I have no place else to go.
— ABRAHAM LINCOLN

ROBERT SCHULLER has been a spiritual adviser to many influential men and women in American politics. Numbered in those ranks are many senators and former presidents.

He told me a story about former President Richard Nixon and former Vice President Hubert Horatio Humphrey that speaks of courage, compassion, forgiveness, and wisdom.

I believe this story stands as a testament to the true spirit of bipartisan politics.

Muriel Humphrey called me and said, "Hubert is now dying. He has only three months to live and we want him to go back to Washington, but he won't do it. If there's one person he would listen to that's you, Reverend Schuller. Can you fly out to Minneapolis?"

So I flew to Minneapolis, and as the plane was landing I am praying, "Oh my God, what am I going to do? How can I possibly convince him?" I was one of the first persons in America, nine years before, whom he took into confidence before he went on television to tell the country he had cancer. For all these years, we've been spiritually together. What would you do, how would you try to talk Hubert

267

Humphrey into going back to Washington? He has only twelve weeks left to live.

I was so upset with myself. I thought, "Oh boy, Schuller, your ego played a trick on you." I was so complimented to be asked to succeed where everyone else failed, that I bit it hook, line, and sinker. What in the dickens can I say to him? And out of the clear blue came a brilliant idea. It was God himself, I am sure, answering my prayer for guidance.

As we sat in his apartment I said, "Hubert, you have had one defeat after another, but you always bounced back." "Yes," he said. I said, "Nixon defeated you by five hundred thousand votes, but you bounced back." "Yes," he said. "How did you always do it?" I asked. When I asked him that question, to answer it he would have to tap into his memory to relive the powerful emotion of that moment in time and it would temporarily revive him.

"Oh," he said, "I looked in my black book. Muriel, where's my black book?" Muriel went and got the black book and he started reading the inspirational sayings of Victor Hugo: "The future has several names: to the fearful, it is terror; to the anxious it is agony; to the men of faith, it's ideal."

And I said, "Hubert, then for you the future is ideal. You go back to Washington one last time." It caught him off guard like a left hook, and the spark got in his eye and he said,

"Yeah. Yeah." Muriel smiled and I thanked God.

He walked me to the car, came back, picked up the telephone, and called President Carter, who was in San Francisco. The next day Air Force One dropped by to pick up Hubert in Minneapolis and took him back to Washington for his last grand hurrah.

After it was all over, the big parties and such, Hubert called and said, "Bob, I want to thank you." I said, "Don't thank me, thank the good Lord, because I didn't know what I was going to do or how to convince you to go back." And he said again, "How can I thank you?" "Well," I said, "maybe I can ask a favor here, if you're not too dead yet to help." "What can I do?" Hubert asked.

And I told him I had another close friend, only he's twenty-one miles away in exile like Napoleon. "Ah," he said. He knew I was talking about Nixon, who at that point had resigned and hadn't been seen in public since the helicopter landed in San Clemente.

I said, "I have a question. Will he ever be able to expose his face in public again? The first time is going to be awful." He said, "That'll be a toughie." I said, "I've been thinking, Hubert, that he can never go out again unless it is to a BIG, national, historic event. It's got to be thrown by a Democrat, not by a Republican. Any Democrat who throws that kind of a party and invites Nixon had better

269

not run for reelection." He said, "I know what you're thinking." I said, "Thank you."

We hung up and Hubert picked up the phone, called Nixon, and invited him to sit next to Muriel when his body would lie in state in the Rotunda in Washington. That's exactly what I had in mind. That was Nixon's first coming-out, sitting next to Muriel. That's an answer to prayer.

I REMEMBER one very interesting intersection of prayer and politics. In 1992, I went to Israel and was standing in front of the Western Wall, my head bowed out of respect for the ancient Wall's purpose.

I sensed someone next to me and looked up to see this guy who looked like he wanted to say something to me. So I gave him one of those "hi, how are ya" nods. He smiles, and I'm expecting him to say how spiritually moved he is by the Wall. He leans in and says in my ear, "How you think Perot's going to do?"

With another set of presidential primaries coming up prior to our next presidential election in the year 2000, I thought it would be a good idea to put some questions about prayer and politics to a few men who might be running for president. Of course, no one has announced intentions as yet, but that's never stopped anyone from speculating on any issue in Washington.

I HAD the chance to talk with Lamar Alexander about his career in politics to date, and about how he uses prayer in his life.

Did you pray before announcing you were going to run for president?

Yes, I prayed for help and to understand what God wanted me to do. My prayers are pretty brief and simple — usually in praise of God and giving thanks. Sometimes I repeat the Psalms. The Twenty-third and the Hundred Twenty-first Psalms are favorites of mine.

Tell me about your prayers during the race for president.

I prayed that God would help me understand what he wanted me to do with my life. That's the prayer I pray most often. I think of my life as a gift from God.

What about when you were governor of Tennessee?

When I was inaugurated, I prayed for understanding and wisdom to do what was right. My brother-in-law, Bill Karl, a minister of the First Presbyterian Church in Dallas, gave the inaugural sermon and used a prayer from Kings I, chapter three, verse nine, which says, "Give therefore thy servant an understanding heart to judge thy people, that I may discern between good and evil." Solomon prayed for this. It reminded me that I am a servant and that I needed an understanding heart to hear both God and the people I am to serve.

Every Sunday in our church we pray for the

president and for the governor and our leaders in office. We pray for them to have wisdom and understanding and to know that they are servants. And when we are in office, I think we pray to remember that we are servants.

Prayer is often a part of making a decision. It is knowing what is right and what is wrong. All facets of our lives are filled with gray areas where some things are right and some things are wrong, and people in public life need the capacity to make the right choices.

Do you pray to get enough votes on election night?

I say prayers on election night when the votes are being counted, but not to win the election. The specific things that I pray for are not that the University of Tennessee wins the football game or that I win the election or that I get enough votes to pass a bill. In those cases, I pray that I will know what God wants to happen.

Define prayer.

It's an opportunity to put aside the world and allow God to fill you up. For someone who has never prayed I would suggest beginning with silence. Just say, "God, help me." That's a good start.

CONGRESSMAN, CABINET secretary, presidential candidate, and former New York Jets quarterback, Jack Kemp says his prayers have been answered when he looks at his family as well as his country. And he prays daily.

What do you say to God?

My wife and I read the Bible and we also read My Utmost for His Highest *by Oswald Chambers. But our favorite family prayer comes from the Book of Proverbs, chapter three, verses five and six: "Trust in the Lord with all thine heart; and lean not unto thine own understanding. In all thy ways acknowledge him, and he shall direct thy paths." That is our spoken and unspoken prayer. It was Solomon, if I understand Proverbs correctly.*

Do you ever feel that your prayers have been answered?

Absolutely.

Have you ever made a bargain with God?

No. I don't make bargains with God. I thank him for my wife of thirty-nine years, our four wonderful children, and eleven grandchildren. I thank him for the blessings to our country. I believe you express your gratitude first before you can be blessed.

What does prayer do for you?

It's a communion with the Holy Father that puts us in touch not only with our own sense of who we are, but also with our neighbors — the respect of treating others as you would want to be treated. That is the ideal. I hope we get closer to it every day.

I WAS at a desk in the CNN office in Washington, on the phone with Irwin. "Maybe I've been around too long, but in the current political climate, what savvy politician would admit that he or she didn't pray? These are powerful people, who spend most of their time fund-raising, and their subordinates poll the public every fifteen minutes to make sure they don't do or say something stupid."

"Don't you think that's a bit cynical?"

"Hey, politics is a brutal and cynical business. You need to have the right answer on the tip of your tongue. I've never met a politician in my life who didn't have all the answers, and now they're all saying, 'Wait a minute, let me check in with the Big Guy'."

"These men aren't asking God to make the decision. They are asking for God's guidance."

"What's the difference?"

"Is it so bad not to have all the answers and to admit that you take time to reflect, to ponder, even to pray for God's help?"

"It would be a lot easier if God would only reveal himself, clearly and plainly."

"Larry, what does the word, 'will' mean to you?"

"The right to choose for myself."

"Exactly. Man was created in the image of God. Unlike his other creations, man was given a unique gift, a divine spark — free will. We have the ability to shape and change the world. If we use our free will correctly, we can beautify and enhance the world. If we misuse it, we plunder and destroy the world."

"That's a big responsibility," I said.

"Maybe that's a reason to check in with the Big Guy?"

Chapter Ten
Prayer and War

In early 1998, before anyone ever knew the name Monica, America was focused on another familiar name: Saddam.

Iraq's resident despot was refusing to allow access for United Nations inspectors to specific sites where it was believed Iraqis were hiding chemical and biological weapons.

It was a tense time as the White House contemplated yet another military action against Iraq. Secretary of State Madeline Albright was traveling through Europe and the Middle East making the case for military intervention if Saddam Hussein continued to refuse access to the sites in question. American servicemen were put on alert in preparation for more combat in the Persian Gulf. Once again, we were a nation on the brink of military conflict.

On a cool February day, the National Cathedral in Washington, D.C., opened Resurrection Chapel on its crypt level for those who wanted to pray. Throughout that day, people filed in and sat for a few moments in the candlelit room, praying or meditating that deci-sion-makers of the United States and the United Nations could find another way to re-solve this crisis other than war.

ONE LEVEL above the chapel, the Reverend Canon Frank Harron, vicar of the cathedral, was speaking to a congregation.

Every war leaves us women and men who carry the scars with them for life. Pray for them. The words of the prayer book seem most helpful: "Strengthen them in their trials and temptations; give them courage to face the perils which beset them; and grant them a sense of your abiding presence wherever they may be. . . ."

But can we also find it in our hearts to pray for the Iraqi people, especially the women and children? If the published reports are true, a conservative estimate by our own gov-ernment is that fifteen hundred people would be killed in Iraq in just four days of bombing. . . . I bid your prayers for our president and his advisers, as well as for the secretary gen-eral of the United Nations, Kofi Annan. These individuals are making critical decisions, even this day, which will affect so many.

As it turned out, those prayers were an-swered. There was no war. Kofi Annan had a face-to-face with Saddam Hussein, and within days the inspections resumed.

During these events, the rabbi and I were at my Arlington place which overlooks the Potomac River and the Lincoln Memorial. It is next door to Fort Meyer as well as the Iwo Jima Memorial. Just down Highway 110 is Arlington National Cemetery, and if you continue past the thousands of white grave markers, the Pentagon is less than a mile away. In Washington, you are never far from a reminder that war is a part of the fabric of our history.

"I remember 1991," I told the rabbi, "and the utter despair I was feeling. I can't understand how a modern society knowing the horrors of war can be on the brink of it again. It makes me angry. If there is a God, then why does he continue to let this happen?"

"War is man's doing, not God's."

"Excuse me? Aren't you the one who told me God clogged my artery to get my attention? If God has nothing to do with war, why are so many people in churches, synagogues, and mosques today?"

"Why are people in churches or synagogues or mosques every day of the week? Larry, we make the decisions. We can choose to talk or we can choose to fight. If you want to walk into traffic, God isn't going to pull you back. A friend or a complete stranger might do it, but God gives you the ability to think and reason. You must decide for yourself. If mankind wills a war, God will allow it."

"If God is all knowing and all loving, why

would he allow a war instead of stopping it?"

"The Bible tells us it is man's responsibility to resist evil, to fight evil and eradicate it. Put these questions to yourself, not God. Do you value morality more than life? Are you prepared to fight for right and good? Hitler, Bosnia, Saddam Hussein are all here to get our attention. God allows them to exist in order to wake us up."

"How can you be so sure of this, Irwin, when the only answer I keep coming up with is 'I don't know'?"

"Quit standing on the sidelines like an interviewer or observer and learn how to participate in your own life. You must choose. There's a saying in Judaism: 'Don't avoid thinking because you might learn something. Don't avoid walking because you might stumble. If you run you might fall and if you try you might fail. So if you don't live you die.' "

There was yet another one of those uncomfortable pauses and I finally said, "Irwin, I just don't know."

"Larry, did I ever tell you the story about the hungry ass equidistant from two bales of hay? It is just as far from the one on the right as it is from the one on the left. You know what happens?"

"It eats both bales?"

"Wrong. It starves to death because it can't make a decision. Larry, you have to choose. You can't always stand in the middle where

'I-don't-know' hangs out because you will die spiritually."

That's when the phone rang. He was getting to me and I don't like it when someone gets under my skin. I can get under other people's skins because that's my job, but this was becoming too personal. The phone kept ringing. I've never been more grateful to hear that horrible sound in my life. If it was a telemarketer they were going to get a double order for the pre-approved Visa card or Sprint phone service and I was certainly going to do an interview with them. I stood to answer the phone on my desk and, as I did, Irwin stood as well.

"It's God," I said. "He calls every week about this time. I would call him, but the toll charges are ridiculous. That's *really* long distance."

Irwin obviously didn't appreciate my feeble attempts at humor. "God calls on prophets, Larry, not talk show hosts," he said, exiting.

IN 1969, a nineteen-year-old boy named Jan Scruggs was spending Memorial Day weekend in a Vietnam jungle, miles away from the provincial capital of Xuan Loc. His group had walked right into a North Vietnamese ambush with the Thirty-third NVA Regiment, and after four hours of fighting, thirteen of his guys were dead or wounded. They remained under fire throughout the night and decided to move out the next morning.

As they did, all hell broke loose and the U.S. forces were pinned by continuous North Vietnamese fire. Scruggs remembers moving to another position just a few yards away, for some reason, and as he did a rocket-propelled grenade landed in the very spot he had been lying, leaving a crater two and a half feet deep by two and a half feet wide. Seconds later there was an incredible explosion, throwing his rifle into the air.

Jan Scruggs had wounds on his shoulder, back, and both legs.

Whoever was shooting at us had us pretty well zeroed in and I realized the firing was not coming from in front of us but from behind us. We were slowly being picked off, one by one. I lay there saying, "I can't do this anymore." I remembered someone telling me if you can move your feet after being hit, then chances are good you won't be paralyzed.

So I did that and then I prayed to God. I started saying I didn't want to die in this terrible hellhole. It was just a place nobody would want to die in. Then I said the Lord's Prayer, and when I finished the pain really started in on me. I said aloud, "F***!" But having been brought up Southern Baptist I knew that wasn't a very good way to end a conversation with God, so I started apologizing. The next thing I knew I was being pulled through the jungle by my legs and placed behind some cover, and I woke up on a helicopter en route *to medical treatment.*

While recovering from his wounds, Scruggs found himself praying for his buddies in the field as well as for his family. He had prayed occasionally in the past, but now he was praying every night and sometimes during the day. Scruggs was quick to say that he doesn't think the prayers after being wounded were any different or more significant than those before he was injured. To this day, however, he has a phone conversation every May 28 with a fellow who was also injured in that incident.

After recovering from his wounds, Scruggs was back in action. More than one doctor told him he was lucky to be alive. In early January of 1970, with only two weeks remaining in his Vietnam tour, someone was working near mortar rounds when there was an explosion.

Jan was the first to arrive at the scene where twelve of his friends lay dead.

I could see men on fire — intestines, brains, body parts, and blood all over the place. And I'm looking at this and standing there with a single bandage that I always carried with me. So I scream for fire extinguishers and medics and I try to bandage one guy from Cleveland, but someone tells me he's gone. A piece of shrapnel had gone right into his brain. That really damaged me. I realized right there that I wanted no part of it anymore.

When Scruggs returned home from Vietnam he was angry over being placed in such an impossible-to-win situation by the American military and he was angry at God. He questioned his relationship with the Almighty for a long time after the war. He participated in what he called a God/prayer boycott.

The questions remained, but Scruggs started attending Protestant services at the Naval Academy in Annapolis, Maryland, as a way of keeping in contact with "the Great Spirit" and he became a driving force behind the planning and implementation of the Vietnam Memorial.

Dear God, please help my little boy to play the part of a man in this infectious blood-poisoning of nations we call war. Give him the gift of thine own forgiveness that he in turn may forgive me and the rest of my generation who stood smugly by and permitted this senseless and insane thing to come about. Give him the strength to hold fast to his little-boy dreams and hopes and aspirations while all the forces of international evil seek to turn him into an efficient and deadly killer. And if thou dost decree that he shall not come back, then let his end be quick and sudden and sharp and not like that of thine only begotten Son who hung upon a cross for long hours far off in Calvary. And give him the inspiration of thine own divine wisdom that he may protect and preserve

the lives of the men he commands who are fathers of little children and the husbands of young wives and the sons of mothers most of whom are older in years than he. For please remember, God, that he is only nineteen and a Second Lieutenant of Infantry in the Army of our United States.

— FATHER'S PRAYER FOR
A SON IN WORLD WAR II

ON AUGUST 7, 1945, a young B-29 pilot was strolling around his aircraft on Tinian Island in the Northern Mariana chain in the Pacific. He looked at Runway A just beyond the airplane and ran the numbers through his head. The runway was 8,500 feet long and, while Charles Sweeney decided he wouldn't need 8,501 feet to get off the ground, it was going to be close.

The B-29 was named *Bock's Car* and in another few days he was going to pilot the aircraft carrying a 10,300-pound payload — an atomic bomb called "The Fat Man, destination Nagasaki." One day earlier, General Sweeney had flown his plane, *The Great Artiste*, off the right wing of the *Enola Gay*, which had dropped the first atomic bomb on Hiroshima.

Did you pray before the Nagasaki mission?

I did pray. After I came back from the Hiroshima mission I had a one-on-one with a Catholic chaplain. He knew about Hiroshima but he wasn't aware I was assigned to the Nagasaki mission. Nobody knew there was going to be another one. I borrowed a Jeep and drove to the 313th Bombardment Wing and I met with the priest who wasn't much older than I. We sat in the open air and I asked, "What do you think?"

He told me it seems Saint Thomas Aquinas struggled with this very situation when he talked about the force of evil. The Japanese attacked us at Pearl Harbor and the killing had to be stopped. He said in that case, as he reads Aquinas, America's efforts to try and stop the war were right.

Thomas Aquinas said war was justified if (1) the intention is to advance the common good, (2) war is declared, and (3) the cause is just.

So God does take sides in war?

It is my feeling God takes no sides in war but, rather, in the forces of evil versus good. I don't think these issues have to be decided by the forces of war, but the human race is less than perfect, and since the Stone Age we have used war to attain our goals. I think God has a special place for the innocent victims of war and I think there's a reason God made suffering in the world — it is to prepare people for a more glorious afterlife.

After the bomb was dropped over Nagasaki, what were your thoughts?

There was a lot of smoke and it took a few days before we saw what had happened, but we had a good sense of what it was. I thought America was slated to win the war sooner or later, but we could have easily lost another half a million men. I was glad I was American. I didn't go off into a corner and sit down with God.

Did you later?

No. I felt anguish for the people, but the cause of their deaths was Tojo and Suzuki. They were getting leaflets saying they would be firebombed and the Japanese warlords wouldn't let them evacuate. I didn't say any double kind of prayer just because this was a different kind of bomb.

Have you always prayed?

I say a prayer before every takeoff. I say, "Jesus, help me." I have been in many situations — approaches in bad weather, mechanical failures, plenty of flying trouble — and I've always said, afterward, "God must have saved me for my children, not for me." My mother and father taught me about morning and evening prayers and I've always done it. I never got out of the habit.

What do you pray for now?

That we don't go to war again. During Desert Storm I prayed we wouldn't put Americans in combat where they were not supposed to be, as in Vietnam.

The will of God prevails. In great contests each party claims to act in accor-

dance with the will of God. Both may be, and one must be, wrong. God cannot be for and against the same thing at the same time. In the present civil war it is quite possible that God's purpose is something different from the purpose of either party; and yet the human instrumentalities, working just as they do, are of the best adaptation to effect his purpose. I am almost ready to say that this is probably true; that God wills this contest, and wills that it shall not end yet. By his mere great power on the minds of the now contestants, he could have either saved or destroyed the Union without a human contest. Yet the contest began. And, having begun, he could give the final victory to either side any day. Yet the contest proceeds.

— ABRAHAM LINCOLN
"MEDITATION ON THE DIVINE WILL"

ALEXANDER HAIG says that being in a war gives you the ability to say a prayer very quickly or, to use his words, "in a flash." He should know, because this former Supreme NATO Commander served in Korea and Vietnam before becoming senior military adviser during the Nixon administration.

I remember the conversation I had with General Haig in January of 1991. President Bush had announced Operation Just Cause, which marked the beginning of the Persian Gulf War. General Haig was sitting with me in the radio studio that evening talking to listeners about events thousands of miles away, but those events were brought to our homes through live coverage by all the television and radio networks. We watched the SCUDs being fired and the Patriot missiles trying to take them out. It didn't occur to me at the time, but all the talking we were doing during that period was probably medicinal.

Talk radio and my television program and even letters to the editor in newspapers allowed people to say, "This scares me," or "This makes me nervous," so all the talking was a good thing. I still remember callers telling General Haig that evening that their prayers were with the troops and the general telling them that every prayer can be used.

We talked with General Haig about his war experiences and he related this incident in 1967, just before the Tet Offensive in Vietnam.

My battalion got into one of the heaviest fights in the war and it was the last major offensive for the U.S. My platoon was pinned down and being decimated by a very large North Vietnamese force in the 179th Regiment. I flew over the fire fight and my helicopter, which we called a bubble roach, was shot down. We swirled down and crashed, and the bubble cracked open. I was right in the middle of the enemy force.

To get out of there, my pilot and I had to run to the perimeter and we were under fire all along the way. I remember bullets going between my legs as I ran. In the last twenty-five yards I saw where our forces were and I dove into that area. I remember thinking to myself, after catching my breath, that anytime in the past five or ten minutes it could have been over, but I'm right here. I just said "thank you." I kept saying it over and over, and that's what you always reflect on. You just know there has to be some kind of guiding hand. A split-second difference decided what was life and what was death.

General Haig says God may have bailed him out a number of times on the battlefield, but God doesn't take sides in war.

I never asked for the other guys to lose. Anybody who has been in combat — and I'm not talking about the periphery, I'm talking about the middle of it — becomes very fatalistic. I never even prayed to God to get me out of this. I think the more important concentration was on the lives of those for whom I was responsible. It's a very heavy burden to command a squadron or a platoon and there's probably no comparable experience in life.

Oh Lord, thou knowest how busy I

**must be this day; if I forget thee do not
forget me.**

— SIR JACOB ASTLEY
BEFORE THE BATTLE OF EDGEHILL (1642)

IN 1991, while I was sitting in the studio with
General Haig talking to a nervous country about
Operation Just Cause, Senator John McCain was
praying in his Capitol Hill office. As a member
of the Senate Armed Services Committee, he
had just been briefed by the White House and
the Pentagon on the details of the invasion to
drive back Iraqi forces.

*First I prayed that there would be a mini-
mum number of young lives lost. I think you
pray that your country's interests will prevail
and that God's will be done. And, of course,
you pray that innocent people will not be
killed. War is the worst of all eventualities and
many tragedies occur, so I was also praying
that it would be over soon. I think war is
something human beings do, but I don't think
God is oblivious to it. God cares about every
living soul residing on this earth.*

This Republican senator from Arizona has
been a frequent guest on my television show.
He is a staunch advocate of campaign reform
legislation and is being considered by some as a
potential candidate for the Republican presidential nomination in the year 2000. Before his
election to the Senate in 1986, Senator McCain

served twenty-two years in the navy. Five and a half years, from 1967 until 1973, were spent as a prisoner of war in Vietnam. Exactly thirty years to the day of this interview, his A-4 Skyhawk jet was shot down over Hanoi.

McCain and I talked about prayers and war.

I had to react as I had been trained to get out of the aircraft. There was no time to pray because any hesitation would have caused me to die. The plane was in a steep dive. But I certainly prayed once I was dragged out of the lake and when I was being beaten severely and tormented by the crowd.

I prayed to live, because there was no certainty that I or the friends I was in prison with would survive. I also prayed for deliverance from prison, but there was a strong caveat to that: only if it was God's will.

McCain based his prayers on a distinction found in the Bible, in Matthew, chapter 22, verse 21, which says, ". . . render unto Caesar the things that are Caesar's and render unto God the things that are God's." Flying the A-4 wasn't working for God.

I felt I was rendering unto Caesar when I flew in combat, so I didn't think it was appropriate to ask God to get me out of a situation that rendering unto Caesar had gotten me into.

During those five and a half years, McCain was beaten by his captors but says he never prayed to die, despite some close brushes with death. For that matter, he never wished ill on those who were doing the beatings. I told him he was a better man than I.

When I was being mistreated by the North Vietnamese, many times I found myself asking to just live one more minute rather than one more hour or one more day. And I know I was able to hang on longer because of the spiritual help that I received through prayer.

I disliked some of them very much because they were very cruel people. But I kept telling myself they were a product of the system — that the Communist system and procedure and policy were making them try to get us to do their will and help them in their war effort. But they had no place in my religion or in my beliefs. I wasn't seeking results, but the strength and courage to do the right thing.

Two years before he was released, John McCain and other POWs wanted to have a church service. It was Christmas and there were thirty or forty other prisoners with him in a large cell. McCain had been appointed the room chaplain.

I was the room chaplain not because of my excessive virtue but because I knew all the prayers that went with a church service, since I had been in boarding school and I was Episcopalian. We asked for a Bible and the Vietnamese said they didn't have any. Later we learned thousands of Bibles had been sent to us.

Four days before Christmas I was told that I could copy prayers and stories from the only Bible the Vietnamese had available. I copied various parts of the Christmas story — selections from Matthew, Mark, Luke, and John — and had a very short time to do it, but I remembered where the stories were.

There was a guy named Quincy Collins who had been director of the Air Force Academy choir and was blessed with a beautiful singing voice. Our service consisted of a biblical passage read by me, followed by an appropriate song by the choir. I talked about the birth of Christ and the choir sang "Silent Night."

I looked around the room and there were tears in those men's eyes. They weren't tears of anger or fright or sorrow or bitterness or even longing for home. They were tears of joy that, for the first time in seven years for some of them, there was a celebration of Christmas together as Americans. It was the most powerful, moving, and remarkable experience I have ever had with prayer.

Tell us about the days before you were released.

When I knew I was going home I prayed that my family was well. I hadn't heard from my family in all those years and I didn't know. When the plane lifted off and we reached water, I said a prayer of thanksgiving. It was a thank-you for allowing me the opportunity to live my life. I have had such a full life, so full of experiences — many of them in the face of death — that I believe I was intended to serve the nation and my fellow citizens.

JAN SCRUGGS, the young infantry man at the beginning of this chapter, worked out his personal demons of the Vietnam War by leading the fight for a fitting memorial to the veterans of that unpopular war. The memorial design finally selected was a simple wall inscribed with the names of all the American soldiers killed in Vietnam.

The design was controversial not only because it was conceived by a young Asian architect, but also because it did not attempt to glorify the war. Many did not feel it was a fitting war memorial.

In January of 1982, Jan Scruggs found himself standing in front of the Shrine of the Immaculate Conception at Catholic University in Washington, D.C., in prayer.

I do believe there is a God and that he will intervene in people's lives. I needed some major assistance with building the Vietnam Memorial. Had I not gone to the war I wouldn't have come up with an idea for the Wall.

After the war I went to college and got a master's degree in psychology and counseling and learned two things: the guilt survivors feel and Carl Jung's idea of the collective un-conscious. We believed that the Wall would help because it can be touched, and that the display of the names of the dead would help heal everyone.

We had some real problems with a fellow named Ross Perot who liked the idea of a memorial for Vietnam but not the design we had selected. I had calls from people like Melvin Laird [defense secretary in the Johnson administration] and Elliot Richardson [attorney general in the Nixon administration] to help me, but I had to go to the Shrine to pray for the project.

It is one hell of a place to pray, just by its hugeness and aura. It puts you in your place. I had been there first while in high school and then in 1979 when my wife, Becky, was very ill and almost died. And I came after my father died. It was always when I had to deal with something.

I asked God to help me against Ross Perot. I was convinced the design was right and the project was right, and it couldn't get tabled because then we'd have to start all over again. Perot wouldn't see it our way so I asked God to help us out. And not long after that prayer, we won. It was a meeting hosted by Senator John Warner that was going to spell up or down for the project. Despite the odds, we came up with a compromise and we got what we wanted. The issue was over *whether there should be a flag or a statue. Remember, the Vietnam Wall was a different kind of memorial. I wanted people to be able to read all of the names. That was a prerequisite.*

Today I think I'm doing with my life what I was meant to do: educate people about the Vietnam War, create the memorial, and maintain its integrity.

The Vietnam Memorial is now the most-visited of all the Washington, D.C., monuments. It displays the names of 58,209 people who died in what was America's longest war — the first American was killed in the Vietnam War in 1959 and the last American died in 1975.

RABBI KATSOF and I were in Arlington again during a stormy Washington night. Our conversations with the soldiers and the generals were at an end. I had interviewed these men on many different occasions, but this time I was moved by the depth of their emotions in recalling their days in combat.

"Do you think what you are feeling could be a message from God?" the rabbi asked.

"Irwin, I'm a pacifist for the most part. I've always believed wars begin when talking stops. As long as two people are talking, there isn't any time to start throwing punches. So if God is trying to teach me something about war, he is preaching to the choir."

The rabbi and I fell into yet another one of our silences. We both stood at the picture window and watched the rain falling on the Potomac and the Lincoln Memorial. Finally I said, "I wonder if we'll ever reach a time when we don't have to build any more war memorials to dead young men."

The rabbi sighed. "God only knows."

Chapter Eleven
Everyday Prayers

Rabbi Katsof was on the phone listening to me explain The Schedule . . .

I had to be in Topeka on Sunday, fly to Los Angeles Sunday night for a CNN taping early Monday morning, and then go to Anaheim where I had a luncheon and a speech, and back to L.A. for a live CNN show that night before flying to Washington on Tuesday to attend a black-tie dinner. All he wanted was five minutes to go over notes, and The Schedule wasn't allowing a thirty-second break.

"Larry, as a rabbi I've had to speak at too many funerals and you know something, not one person ever had an epitaph that said 'He should have spent more time at the office.' If it all ended tomorrow, what would they say about you?"

"If it all ended tomorrow? I've never considered the possibility. Well, let me see . . . we'd have three taped shows and we could probably air some old interviews that aren't time-sensitive. I'd say we could cover the first week."

The rabbi was quiet and I knew what he was

doing. He finished his silent prayer. "Okay," he said, "I'm glad you are covered for the first week. You have answered my question by not answering my question. Larry, look at your life. You have an inner life and you have an outer life. You spend a lot of time in the outer life. You go all over the country, but you don't go anywhere *inside*. You don't listen to The Self, you listen to your work. Prayer does The Self.

"A teacher I know, Rabbi Volbe, says prayer is 'sudden quietness.' It only takes a moment. Take your Self off the road and inspect your vehicle, like the pilot does before he takes off to fly you to Los Angeles."

"Topeka," I corrected him. "I gotta be in Topeka Sunday before Los Angeles."

"Larry, the point is that the pilot first looks around for any problems, because once he's in the air, it's too late. You should do the same thing. Take a quiet moment to see what needs fixing or how you can do things better and, if nothing else, put your feelings into words. You will feel better and that, in turn, will be reflected in your life and your work. Just say thanks. That's always a good beginning."

"How often do you do that?" I asked.

"All the time. But I'll tell you about one time that stands out. After my wife and I had our first four children . . ."

"Four?"

"Didn't we talk about this?"

"Not about four."

"Well, we have seven now . . ."

"Seven? You don't watch much TV, do you? Seven children. It's like Eddie Foy — it's a movie."

"I'm trying to tell a story here. After we had our first four children and they were all under the age of four . . ."

"Four under four?"

"We suffered three miscarriages in a row, one after another for the next three years. We were both very upset, as you can imagine. I did a lot of praying because I didn't understand why this was happening. We were grateful for the four wonderful children we had, but we wanted more. So we did a little self-survey together. I realized I was a workaholic and, if I continued to be one, it would not be healthy for my family."

"So this was one of those learning situations, to shake you up in order to wake you up?"

"Exactly. We saw the problem and made the correction. It took awhile, but we saw it. Then my wife got pregnant again."

"I appreciate your candor, but why are you telling me this?"

"So you will stop trying to be everywhere at once. How will people talk about you, Larry? I know they'll talk about your interviews, your conversations, and all the powerful people you knew, but will anyone say Larry was a happy guy with inner peace who could be alone with himself?"

"People will say a lot of things . . ."

"What would you say?"

"I don't know."

"Larry, you really need to look inside, to do a walkaround. Let me tell you a folk tale."

"A folk tale. That's rabbi-ese for another short story?"

"You'll like this one. When we were in the womb, the angel came and taught us all there is to know about reality. Then just before we were born, the angel touched us underneath our nose, on that little indentation right over our lips, and we forgot everything we had learned. Our job in life is to get back in touch with that knowledge, to look inside ourselves. All that knowledge is within, and the best way to find it is to put your finger over that indentation to remind yourself that if you are silent, if you are quiet, you will figure it out."

I told the rabbi I would take his suggestion and do a walkaround. So after we hung up I took a long look at The Schedule. The afternoon was free. I unhooked the phone, walked around the couch a couple of times, then lay down and took a long, peaceful, quiet nap.

Once in a friend's home I came across this blessing, and took it down in shorthand . . . it says something I like to live with: "Oh thou, who dwellest in so many homes, possess thyself of this. Bless the life that is sheltered here. Grant that trust and peace and comfort abide

within, and that love and life and useful-
ness may go out from this home forever."
— LADY BIRD JOHNSON
ON HER FAMILY'S HOME, CBS TV,
AUGUST 12, 1964

THE RABBI'S concept of the walkaround has
been used a lot. Actor Lou Diamond Phillips
and his wife, Kelly, wanted children in their lives
and said prayers together every day for this to
happen. They tried for more than two years and
during that time spent countless hours of reflection and self-examination. The Phillipses did a
walkaround.

Do you feel prayer played a role in your
wife's getting pregnant?

*It was a very difficult conception. We had
specialists involved, and every month you
would get your hopes up and they would sort
of fall. And we would speak of it honestly in
religious tones. We are not a religious family,
a church-going family, but I do feel that we
are a very spiritual family.*

*I think our babies are a miracle. I think
there was my wife's faith and the strength
that gave her. I know she prayed and lit candles quite often.*

For how many years were you trying to have
children?

*Two and a half years. A friend of ours, a
poker buddy, knew what we were going*

through and he gave us some holy water, blessed by the Pope, that belonged to his mother. We put the holy water on Kelly's stomach around Christmas and in January we were pregnant.

It wasn't until I had the babies here in my arms, and my buddy was back at the poker table, that I put two and two together. I said, "Anthony, when did you give me that holy water? It was Christmas, wasn't it?" I thought, "Ahh! One more link in the chain of faith that brought these little girls to life."

We are in the process of trying to find a faith to raise our children in. It's very important that they have a foundation, a place to start. One of the problems I have with organized religion is that it can be separatist — not acknowledge other people's faiths. We have so many faiths in this country. Multiply it by those around the world — we are living in a global environment. I feel it would be wrong to close their minds.

The rabbi and I interviewed Lou Diamond Phillips one month after his daughters were born. That's right, daughters. They had twins.

THE WALKAROUND was also done at the Jenner household. When the former Olympic decathlon champion married his wife, Kris, they each had four children of their own from previous marriages. And while both were grateful for what they had, Bruce and Kris wanted a legacy to continue their union long after each of them were gone. Another child was the way to do that.

When both of us looked at the fact we had four children each, we agreed it would be easy. Two and one-half months later my wife had a miscarriage. It was the most devastating thing any family can go through. You hear about it all the time, but when you have prayed so hard and it's gone, you are absolutely devastated. It is part of you.

Prayer was important not only to have another child, but prayer was important to get through not having this child. It was prayer for strength. It was a prayer for this little life that we'll never know. And it was a prayer of just sorrow. It wasn't easy to start again.

It was at this point in the interview with Jenner that a child's voice came on the phone. It was his daughter Kendall — the result, according to Bruce, of prayers from the Jenner family and some serious walking around.

I think when there is a tragedy and you are having a difficult time, that it is natural to say maybe there's a better way to lead your life. I know that both my wife and I said to God, "If we do a few things can you take care of this part?" We said, "Well this isn't working and this hurts and what if we do something else that is good?"

We wouldn't have had the miscarriage if

there wasn't something wrong. Obviously something wasn't right. It might have been the baby or the situation or the timing. Maybe we were supposed to work harder. It took another year, but our prayers were answered.

And, by the way, Kendall now has a new baby sister.

RABBI MARVIN HIER, director of the Simon Wiesenthal Center, told us a story about conception.

The story is told of two Orthodox Jews who were childless and were very concerned about it. Being Orthodox Jews who place great faith in prayer and also in going and seeking the blessing of a holy man, these two men go to see a rebbe. They tell the rebbe their problems and hope that the rebbe can beseech God that they be granted children. And the rebbe prayed for them.

He said a prayer for both men. "May God in his infinite compassion grant you each a child within the coming year."

A year went by. One wife was pregnant and a baby boy was born. The other man remained childless and he was frustrated. They both went to the same rebbe, they both said the same prayer. For the first man it worked and for the second it didn't.

The second man went back to the rebbe and he was very angry. He said, "You know, I think it's tremendously unfair of God. I can't understand how it's possible to place my whole faith in God and look what happens. You give us both a blessing, my friend has a child, and I have nothing."

And so the rebbe said to him, "You want me to tell you the difference between you and your friend?"

"Yes, tell me the difference," the second man demanded.

"Okay, you force me to, so I will. When I gave the blessing to both of you, you know what happened, the difference between you and your friend? You went home and your friend went with his wife and they bought a carriage."

To say a prayer is not enough. One has to believe that it is possible for that prayer to be heard. If one just tosses out a prayer, saying, "Well, it's harmless. What can I lose?" but really has no faith in the prayer, no absolute belief in it in the first place, then it will not be answered.

ALAN DERSHOWITZ prayed seven times a day as a child. He continues to be spiritual, praying several times a week. Prayer by this well-known defense attorney brings his household together.

It's a very important part of our family. I do formal prayer every Friday night with my family. I bless my daughter in the traditional

306

way. I put my hand on her head, and I change the prayer a little bit. I don't only bless her that she should be like the famous women of the Bible, I intersperse the names of the men and women I would like her to be like. I talk about the great women and men throughout history, and we usually have a discussion about it. It's the beginning of an interesting weekly discussion about what she's done and what she would like to do.

We use traditional blessings as a way of marking important events. I think that's a form of prayer. It's also a form of family communication. I think of a lot of those prayers as more directed toward my daughter and my wife and my family than necessarily toward heaven. But we know we are praying to something beyond us. When I do it with my family it's a very different experience than when I do it alone.

FILM CRITIC and national radio talk show host Michael Medved says prayers have helped him teach his children good manners.

Look, I think our kids are better kids because they don't grab a candy bar without saying a blessing. I think they're better kids 'cause they check the candy-bar wrapper to see if it's kosher. But I also think that, even more fundamental, is the notion that you teach every child, "Say thank you." Every parent in the world wants to teach his or her child to say thank you.

Teaching children to say a blessing over everything they eat is a way of teaching them, in the most profound sense, to say thank you, because obviously you may need to say thank you to Grandma or to Uncle Morris or someone, but even more than that, you need to say thank you to the source of all gifts.

The aspect of prayer which I think is the most important of all — and I see this with my kids — is blessings, saying blessings over little things. Over the first cereal they eat in the morning they say a blessing and over the new day they say a blessing. In our family we're very good at thanking God for the opportunity to face a new day.

We have the expectation that we should rise up like a lion for the service of the Lord. It doesn't say rise up and whine. It doesn't say rise up and feel self-pity. It doesn't say rise up and count your aches and pains and all the difficulties you have. It says rise up like a lion. A lion is fairly aggressive and knows what has to be done.

Thirty-four percent of Americans say grace occasionally before a meal. Twenty-nine percent always say grace.
— LIFE MAGAZINE SURVEY ON PRAYER, WITH GALLUP ORGANIZATION (DECEMBER 17, 1993)

BILL MOYERS tells a story about his years as press secretary in the Johnson administration. One afternoon he joined the president for lunch at the White House and was asked to say grace. As he began, President Johnson interrupted and started yelling, "I can't hear you! Speak up!" Bill Moyers looked at the president and said, "I wasn't talking to you."

KENNY ROGERS has a tale about the way his grandfather used to say grace.

It's funny how certain things are synergistic to families. My grandfather used to say a prayer at every meal. He was a Pentecostal and he said a prayer before we ate and it was always the same one, but he always used the wrong word. It was no big deal, but it was grammatically incorrect and everyone in my family would always try to correct him and then we'd end up in this big argument.

> We thank thee, Heavenly Father
> for this food that's been prepared
> for the nourishment of our bodies.
> Help us to spend the strength
> that we *arrive* in doing good
> and keeping thy command.
> — BYRD ROGERS
> (the word should be "derive")

My grandfather would say, "You are about

the thirtieth person that's tried to tell me the word is wrong, but this is how my father taught me and I'd appreciate it in the future when you say the prayer that you do it the way I taught you." That we always say the prayer that way makes my family, which is pretty scattered, close.

Kenny Rogers says the prayer at mealtime the same way his grandfather taught him. And today, when Rogers says grace, his children are continually trying to correct his grammar.

DR. LAURA SCHLESSINGER, best-selling author of *Ten Stupid Things Women Do to Mess Up Their Lives* and *How Could You Do That?*, made the cover of *Time* in 1997. She hosts one of the nation's most popular radio shows, where she dispenses advice to people trying to cope with themselves or their mates or their friends and everything that falls in between. She is quick to tell callers, when appropriate, that they are out of their minds. And she doesn't condone sex before marriage, which seems to be the reason a lot of her callers pick up the phone.

She prefaced her conversation with us by saying, "I am a work in progress." Rabbi Katsof looked at me, and said, "You think *you're* a work in progress? Look who I'm with."

Dr. Schlessinger says she doesn't pray often — God has more important matters — but she recalled the time her son gave her a spiritual lesson.

There are times when I feel in a pinch and I'll say, "Oh God, can you help me with this?" and then it immediately comes into my mind there's some kid dying of cancer and I'm not going to busy him with something for which I really have to take responsibility.

But in early 1997 I got very sick and lost my voice, and I was hysterical because this is my means of making a living. And one day I pushed it and I wasn't supposed to talk for two weeks and I got very angry. My son was in the kitchen with me, and I said, "How can God do this? I think I'm doing God's work and he zaps my voice! So where is God now?" And I opened the kitchen cabinet door where the dishes are and I said, "God? You there?" Now, I'm choking this out because I can't even talk, and I sit down and start crying.

My son, who is eleven, comes over and says, "God acts in mysterious ways and right now he's acting through Daddy and me taking care of you." That drained me. I had to go to bed after that, it was such an over-whelming emotional experience. And, eventually, I got my voice back.

My son, Derek, is in Hebrew school, so he's coming home with all the prayers and he's way ahead of me. He teaches me things. I like saying the prayers every day. The blessings. I like that they're not greedy.

What do you mean by that?

Gimme as opposed to thank you. I think people's lives would be immediately im-proved, with each other, much less with God, if their conversations were based on gratitude rather than gimme. Nothing is ever going to be perfect. I don't think God is there for me personally, to help me out with something specific, other than through motivation and inspiration.

God gives you the inspiration?

. . . and motivation, but not stuff. God will not fix my car.

How do we fit into the whole picture?

Well, this is God's creativity. I take the cove-nant very seriously, that we are here to per-fect the world. I think it's predominantly our responsibility at this point, which is why I de-spair sometimes. [Laughter] I think we need a good flood, don't you?

After that interview, Irwin and I were talking about Dr. Laura's experiences with prayer and I mentioned how refreshing it was to hear someone say they weren't sure. And the rabbi said at least she was struggling with her faith.

> **Some pray to marry the man they love,**
> **My prayer will somewhat vary.**
> **I humbly pray to heaven above**
> **To love the man I marry.**
> — ROSE PASTOR STOKES,
> "MY PRAYER"

DR. JOHN GRAY, the best-selling author of *Men Are from Mars, Women Are from Venus*, was facing a major problem in his personal life and worried it would eventually affect his professional life. He and his wife were a successful relation-ship-counseling team and were just beginning to make a name for themselves through their seminars. Together they had developed an interesting and unique approach to improving the interaction between couples. Their seminars were booked months in advance as people came to them for guidance about getting along with their mate.

This positive was offset by a negative, and considering what they did for a living, it was a big one — he and his wife were not communicating. Gray's wife didn't want to have children and he did. They couldn't work through the conflict.

Finally, they separated and filed for divorce.

The divorce was devastating for me. Here I was teaching seminars with my wife — hundreds of people were coming to us around the country and we were scheduled in six different cities to conduct the seminars — and now I had to walk in alone and say I have separated from my wife, thank you for spending your money and time with me to teach you about relationships. I'm thinking to myself, "Why should these people even show up? Why should they listen to anything I say?" So I prayed to God for the strength to do it, but also for clarity as to whether or not I should even go through with it.

Then I walked out that first afternoon in front of everybody and told them that my wife and I were at an end. I asked people why they came and they said their friends had told them about me, and I said they should trust their friends if they can't trust me. I came away from this experience feeling I had been able to help others even though something had been missing in my own marriage.

So I'm going along and staying above water and I get a call from a friend who says the seminar is great, but why can't I teach about the differences between men and women? My first reaction was this guy is sexist. I wasn't open at all to the whole idea. But I started doing research and learned very quickly the problems in my marriage were that we really didn't understand that men and women are different. I started using this in my seminars, and that became the basis for the book Men Are from Mars, Women Are from Venus.

We asked John Gray if he had any advice for single people.

I have a procedure that helps single people, through prayer, find their soul mate. Your soul mate is the partner with whom you can experience true and lasting love for a lifetime. Soul mates are perfect for you, but they're never perfect people.

You have to be honest in the moment. You can't walk around acting like everything is completely perfect in your life and you're completely content without a partner. At the same time, you can't be desperate and needy. There's something in-between where you trust that the right person will come to you at the right time, but you have to honor your feelings that say, "I'm lonely. I'm afraid that I'll never find the right person."

To find this perfect person for you, you have to feel the longing. You have to really want this person in your life: I want to share my life. I want to go to the park and go for a walk with my wife. I want to have children. I want a loving family. You have to clearly create the picture of what you want — with all the details, how it will feel — and then you imagine having that. And then you thank God.

You set the intention, you set the good feelings, and that person comes to you. When they come to you, you will recognize who they are. Without that prayer, the right person may be knocking on your door all the time, and you keep missing him or her because your heart is not open.

PETER LOWE is a successful businessman who organizes seminars around the world, featuring well-known speakers such as Colin Powell, President Bush, and former Surgeon General C.

Everett Koop. The bottom line, which is taught in every Lowe seminar, is that success is attainable and available to everybody.

Lowe told me that prayer is the most important way to prepare for the future. He calls prayer "the planting of the seed," and while it is unreasonable to expect a seed to become a plant the day after it's planted, that doesn't mean the seed isn't growing.

One night Peter Lowe was in his hotel room and realized how empty his life had become, and so he planted a seed. He said a prayer for a wife.

I was in Los Angeles. It was March 8, 1985, at 11:00 P.M. I was praying to God and said, "Anytime I've listened to you regarding my work, career, writing, it has always been right. It may not have seemed right immediately, but looking back six months from whenever I have said a prayer, the answer has been right."

I told God that I'd made a list of twenty-five things I'd like in a wife and I'd yet to meet anyone with even six of these qualities, and I was getting discouraged. Slowly I began to realize that the twenty-five things that are important today may not mean much forty years from now. So I asked God to select the best person for me and let her know right now that I'm thinking about her.

I learned later that a woman in New Orleans had woken up at that moment from a

*dream that she was going to meet her hus-
band-to-be. We met several months later and
compared journals and notes, and there it
was — the exact same time in both. And she
has all twenty-five things I originally wanted.*

*I was attending a writers' conference and I
was late for one of the sessions. Right before I
went into the lecture, I heard God speak to
me and I was told my wife-to-be is on the
other side of the door that I was about to go
through. I married the woman on the other
side of that door.*

Peter Lowe says prayer is "the gymnasium of
the soul." He says that he works out his soul
when he prays.

DAVID SACKS, co-executive producer of *3RD
Rock from the Sun*, also prayed for a wife.

*I prayed for a wife for a long time. And that
prayer was definitely answered. But it took
years and a lot of tears. I looked back on my
life and I wanted to know why it took so long.
And I realized that when I was praying for it
initially, I wasn't in the right place to receive
the maximum benefit.*

*A lot of people are confused and discour-
aged when God's answer to a prayer is no.
They think if what they pray for in particular
doesn't manifest itself immediately, that this is
somehow a rejection of their attempt to draw
close. That isn't the case. God is guiding us re-*

gardless. The trick is to be more aware, more sensitive, and more connected — to understand that even when we feel thwarted, this is an act of kindness on the part of God.

I heard a beautiful story about a rabbi who had just buried his son. We shouldn't know from such tragedies, but he came back from the funeral, went to shul, and started crying out in praise of God. Someone said to him, "What's going on? You just buried a child. How can you react like this? You seem so happy." He said, "When I experienced this tragedy, I felt like I was hit very, very, very hard on the back. When I turned around to see who had done it, I saw it was my best friend."

BARBARA DE ANGELIS is a motivational speaker and relationships expert. She is a best-selling author with numerous books to her credit and runs her own company, Shakti Communications. Shakti is a Sanskrit word which Barbara says is comparable to the Tao, energy, or soul. For those of us weaned on pop culture, shakti is the "force" that Luke Skywalker was always talking about in the *Star Wars* movies.

Is there a difference between prayer and meditation?

Meditation is the opposite of prayer. It is one end of the conversation and prayer is the other. Meditation is the reception, the listen-

ing, the opening, and prayer is the connecting out, the asking. I think there are different kinds of prayer. There are the original prayers — praise and gratitude. In these, you are not asking, begging, pleading, or looking for an answer as much as honoring and thanking. I thank God for my life, for another day, the ability to serve.

Praying is saying thank you?

That form of prayer, yes. In our civilization in the last century, a lot of people seem to think of prayer only as pleading or begging, such as, "Dear God, please help me get this job and I'll be good." Prayer has become a business transaction — it's spiritually immature. I think of it this way: I am an expression of God, I am a piece of God. Every morning I say an ancient Hindu prayer: "May my mouth be a channel for your words, may my hand serve as your hand, may my heart serve as your love, may my action reflect you."

It connects me back to my source and it gets me out of the way. When I write, if I'm really allowing God to participate completely, as opposed to my ego and my intellect, there's a lot of shakti. It isn't on the page but it can come through the page. People come up to me and say, "I was reading your book and I got such a rush and I felt so loved by you." I know they're really saying, "I felt the shakti."

That's the true role of a teacher — to help

319

you awaken your own greatness, your own soul.

ANTHONY ROBBINS travels the world talking to corporations and holding seminars on success. Like Barbara De Angelis, Robbins takes a moment to pray before going in front of an audience.

I pray quietly. Usually, I try to find a place where I can be alone, but that isn't always possible so I will just say a prayer to myself just before going on stage. It's always the same message and the same thought. It's always use me . . . use me . . . use me. I ask for guidance, but then I have to go do the work. My prayer is always for God to let me connect to being stronger — to use me for a greater good. It is not, "Make it easier."

I don't believe in waiting for winter to start praying for spring or for the night to begin praying for the day. What you hold in your heart will seek its level.

DENNIS PRAGER is one of America's most respected radio talk show hosts. He has been broadcasting on KABC Radio in Los Angeles for fifteen years.

His book *Think a Second Time* was praised by William Bennett as "one of those rare books that can change an intelligent mind." He has been lecturing for almost ten years on the subject of his most recent book — *Happiness Is a Serious Problem*.

What is the relationship between prayer and happiness?

The most important component of happiness, by far — there isn't a close second — is gratitude. Nothing instills gratitude as much as religion and prayer done correctly. Prayer is a major vehicle to gratitude. Not request prayer, grateful prayer: Thank you, God. My favorite holiday is Thanksgiving, the day of gratitude to God.

This is a ballpark question: What is your understanding of our role in the universe?

Our role in the universe — it's not original to me — is completing God's work by using our free will to be good and holy, to make a better world than we have inherited, to appreciate what we've been given, and to enjoy it. I am absolutely convinced it is a sin to be unhappy. A big sin. It's a statement to God that he blew it.

ONE QUESTION I asked everybody was never planned in advance. The rabbi and I were in another traffic jam on Sunset Boulevard. I was supposed to meet Shawn and some friends for dinner after my CNN show and I was ten minutes away from Spago in Beverly Hills. My reservation was for ten minutes ago.

We're at a traffic stoplight and it seems as though it just won't change. It stays red. I'm going nuts. I'm phoning the restaurant and saying I'm running late, hold the table, seat everyone even if I'm not there. And then I'm hitting the seat with my hands and then I'm rolling down the window and yelling at nobody in particular and, well, as the rabbi said, "It wasn't pretty." I even call the L.A. cops to complain about the traffic. You know, sometimes you can talk and it feels like nobody's listening.

"Larry, it's just a traffic light. Relax."

"This is driving me nuts," I said. The light stayed red. Horns were honking and the rabbi was serene and tranquil and calm as I raged against the injustice of it all. "I wish there was something I could do," I mumbled. That's when the rabbi pointed to the car next to us. The driver was a small woman with brown hair. She was wearing a sweatshirt and in her hands was a rosary. She was praying.

"You want to try it?" Irwin asked. "Couldn't hurt . . ."

"Is God also in charge of traffic lights? I don't think so."

"God is in charge of everything, as I will illustrate."

"Do I feel another short story approaching?"

"There was this writer who was irritated whenever an ambulance or fire engine passed his house. It would interrupt his concentration to the point of frustration and then he couldn't get back to work. So he prayed about it and received an answer. Now whenever an ambulance or a fire engine passes, he says a prayer in hopes that the ambulance gets to the hospital in time to save the patient and the fire engine to the house that's on fire.

"The writer says positive and negative thoughts can't be in the same room any more than light and dark can be in one room. So if you are annoyed when you hear that siren, turn it into a positive by praying for the patient in the ambulance or the person whose house is on fire. The writer was able to turn his irritation into a positive."

"So, using your logic, we are backed up at this stoplight and I'm getting irritated, but I shouldn't because there is someone else in Los Angeles who needs to be somewhere before me."

"Perhaps."

"All right, Rabbi, but I want to know what's more important than a reservation at Spago?"

Before Rabbi Katsof could answer, the light turned green and we started moving forward. "Thank God," I said, not thinking. I was about to backtrack but Irwin beat me to it.

"I thought you said God doesn't do traffic lights."

For one of the few times in my adult life, I was at a loss for words. His logic was too strong.

I PUT the stoplight question to Chuck Colson.

I don't think praying for the light to change is a good use of prayer. Remember, you are praying for God's will and God's will may not be your will. So if I'm sitting at a traffic light and there is someplace I have to be, I would pray for patience while I wait for the light to change. That's the better way to do it.

Now, that said, I'll tell you a story. There was a time I was on Capitol Hill to see a senator and I was late. I couldn't find a parking place. I went around and around and there was nothing. I said, "God, help me out here." I turned the corner and there was a parking place.

THE DAY I went to interview Virginia Harris, the chairman of the Christian Science board of directors, was the same day the Washington, D.C., government decided to make all the one-way streets run in the opposite direction.

Not only that, but they also put those paper bags over half the parking meters, which means "no parking." I had a 9:00 A.M. appointment and at 9:06 A.M. I still hadn't found a place to park. So you know what the first question was.

Have you ever prayed for a parking spot?

My kids used to laugh because every time I prayed for one I'd find one, and then I would pray there was money in the meter.

I think if you are praying to beat someone

out of a parking place, that would be wrong. Look at your motive and you'll find the answer to the question. If you are doing something that you are supposed to be doing, then there's nothing wrong with asking God to help you out. If you pray to beat someone out of a job, then that's wrong.

PAT PIPER, producer of my radio show when I was with Mutual Broadcasting, and I used to travel across the country almost every month to do live programs in cities where we had an affiliate. At one point we had more than four hundred radio stations carrying the program.

We traveled together only once, and after that flight from Washington's Dulles airport to LAX in Los Angeles, Pat started booking himself on AFBL — Any Flight But Larry's. Now, to my knowledge, nobody has ever prayed to make sure they don't end up on the same flight with me, but then I've never polled the passengers and, quite frankly, that's an answer I don't care to know.

But it is the sound basis for another travel question: Do you pray in the airport before a flight?

WE ASKED Aaron Spelling that question and got an interesting answer.

Aaron Spelling, executive producer of *Char-*

lie's Angels, *Beverly Hills 90210*, and *Melrose Place*, never flies. He told me that when he was in the army, because of a cold a doctor refused to let him fly on a three-day pass to see his mother. A few hours later that plane crashed, killing everyone on board, and the air force told his family that he was dead.

By the time Aaron arrived there were cars all around the house. He was worried because his family didn't own a car and the only time cars were at their house was after a funeral, a death, or a marriage. He rushed in, and when his mother saw him she passed out. She made him promise to never fly again.

He has kept that promise, but when his wife or children fly, Aaron makes sure to say a prayer.

I always take them to the airport and I pray they get there safely. The one rule in our family is to call from the airport after you land. I pray when that plane takes off and I say, "Please God, let them arrive safely," and I repeat this about two times in my head. Then, when I get the phone call, I know my prayers have been answered.

CAL THOMAS considers praying for a parking place a trivial exercise, but flying is a different matter altogether.

I pray before every takeoff. I do it every time. There is no exception. I pray just as I get on the plane and I pray through the storms. I pray for the pilot and the co-pilot and the air traffic controllers. But when we hit the bad weather — you know, when the plane is shaking and you are going through those huge potholes in the sky — I don't sit there saying prayers out loud. I read the newspaper, but I'm not reading it at all. I'm praying.

MARK VICTOR HANSEN, one of America's foremost authorities on personal growth and potential and co-author with Jack Canfield of the phenomenal best-selling book *Chicken Soup for the Soul*, and others, told us:

I would never start a day without praying. I wake up and use the Old Testament line, "This is a day the Lord has made and I shall rejoice and be glad in it." In my prayer time, I take God's eyes, look through my heart, and I say, "What would God look at today if God were trying to make this a really magnificent day, one that made a difference and contributed in a significant and important way?"

FORMER GOVERNOR of Texas, Ann Richards, says she prays through the day, but . . .

I always pray before I go to sleep. And I try to guard against the prayer at the end of the day becoming a mantra. Mantras are powerful, but prayer can't be something done by rote. Prayer needs a conscious connection. I routinely use the Lord's Prayer. Then I review the day and express thanks for the good things that have happened.

But I've never prayed that God should alleviate my situation or take away the difficulty. I've never looked on God as being a large eraser. I've always prayed for the strength to deal with it myself. I don't think you ask God to do it for you. The most powerful prayer, and my most favorite, is the serenity prayer: "God, grant me the wisdom to accept the things I cannot change, the courage to change the things I can, and the wisdom to know the difference."

I hope that's what I practice. God only asks us to do our best, not to be perfect, and that prayer says, "I'm going to be as level about this as I can. And I'm going to be serene in my approach, and where I can do something I am going to do it and do it courageously. I pray to God to be granted the wisdom to know the difference."

VIRGINIA HARRIS says an important part of her prayer practice is creating the right place for it to happen.

I have a little corner where I can look out the windows and let my thoughts out and in while sitting in an easy chair. I look at the huge pine trees and the sky in Boston and look at the seasons and the colors. I've always had my little nest where I pray. In every home my husband and I have ever lived in, I've always found one.

I don't try to direct my thoughts when I pray. I read a book of prayers and I say, "This is the word of God and this is God's message to me today." I think about who I am and what I am. Where do I go next? God is in the details.

Then at night when I'm in bed I take a moment and go through the day. Did I square my account with God? What more do I have to do? Could I have done something different? I've always established through the prayer in the morning a connection to God, so it doesn't turn off or stop. Sometimes I think he is sitting here on my shoulder.

Let everyone try and find that as a result of their daily prayer he adds something new to his life, something with which nothing can be compared.

— MAHATMA GANDHI

MANY YEARS ago, a guy walked into my radio studio dressed in a long robe. He had a thick, lengthy beard and his hair fell freely on his shoulders. An engineer who worked that shift was very excited about this guest and was clearly finding all kinds of excuses to stay in the studio. He motioned for me to meet him in the hallway, which I did.

"I can't believe he's your guest tonight," he told me. "Gibbons is the best guitar player in the world!"

I hadn't checked the line-up for the evening and didn't even know the guy's name. I like to be spontaneous, so I never plan out many interviews in advance. In fact, this evening I hadn't even read the biographical information that had been provided me by my producer, but this engineer seemed to know everything about our guest.

"Larry, he's a member of a great Southern rock band and they have hit after hit after hit. ZZ Top is the best and I didn't know they were even in town." I thanked him for the information and went back into the studio to watch the baseball game on television. The Orioles were losing.

My guest was sitting there with his eyes closed, looking to me like he had just arrived from another planet. That got me to wondering if I was going to have a loony-tune on my hands for the next two hours.

One minute before air we did the standard microphone check and I made some small talk, asking how the tour was going and how long he was going to be in town, and all the time I didn't have a clue who ZZ Top was.

The show's theme started rolling and I opened my package of information about the guest and learned suddenly that he was NOT

Billy Gibbons of ZZ Top, but Swami Satchidananda. He was born in India and in 1966 came to the United States where he founded the Integral Yoga Institute, now with over forty chapters. The international headquarters is in Buckingham, Virginia.

Obviously, the engineer didn't know what he was talking about. Which meant that at that very moment, I didn't have a clue what I was going to talk about. So I started the conversation with the obvious question, "Did you know you're a dead ringer for Billy Gibbons of ZZ Top?"

"I don't know who that is," was the polite answer. "What is a ZZ?"

"Top," I finished the sentence for him. "It's not important," I said, trying to cover my losses which were quickly piling up.

We kept talking and the swami turned out to be one of my most memorable guests ever. Even the engineer came up to me after the show and said he liked what he heard. I figure it like this: if the engineers like what they hear, everyone else is going to as well.

The swami started in right away. "When you opened your eyes today, Larry, what did you think?"

"Nothing, I didn't think anything."

"Not a 'thank you'?"

"Nope."

"Are you entitled to this day?"

"Hey, I woke up so, yeah, I'm a part of it."

"But if you said thank you, then you would be a part of the whole day, wouldn't you? You can just show up or you can be a part of it. Let's try it this way: you go to the deli and you order toast and it comes out burned. What do you do?"

"I start yelling. I paid for toast."

"And what good does yelling do?"

"Maybe it gets me better toast."

"Larry, you need to go to the kitchen and thank them for the toast. You need to let them know how grateful you are for the toast. And then you need to ask if there might be any that isn't burned and offer to take the bad toast and make sure it doesn't go to waste."

I had nothing to say to the swami. Everyone in the control room was in hysterics.

"Well, Swami, if I yell, I have let them know they screwed up and I've let them know I'm not to be taken advantage of, and there's always the threat I'll walk out and not pay, since they made the mistake."

"But you are ruining the air between you and the person doing the toast," the swami said. "You should be grateful to have had the chance to offer a solution and, possibly, leave the deli better than when you walked in. That is the difference between just showing up and leaving, and participating."

THE LEARNING curve differs from person to

person, but I figure we are all works in pro
I told my swami story to the rabbi at o
"prayer meeting" at the corner of Broadw
Fifty-seventh, a few blocks from my culinary an-
cestral home — the Carnegie Deli.

"A very wise man, very wise!" Irwin said as
he took a silent moment and looked at me in-
tently. "So, Larry, we are done. Tell me, do you
pray now?"

"No, I don't pray."

"Have you thought about trying?"

"Oh, you know, I've made it sixty-plus years,"
I said, "and it would be uncomfortable to start
now. But, it has been one hell of a journey and
I'm glad to have been part of the adventure."

Irwin took a sip of Diet Snapple. "Let me understand this, you are glad to have been a *part*
of the adventure?"

"That's right, Irwin."

"You may have listened to the swami, Larry,
but I don't think you heard him."

I knew what was coming. "Short story,
right?"

"A short one and also the last one. These
three farmers are out in a field, down on their
knees, looking up at the heavens. A fourth
farmer walks up and asks them what they're
doing. They tell him they're praying for rain.
And the fourth farmer says, 'Nope, I don't
think so.' And the first farmer says to him, 'Of
course, we're praying. We are down on our
knees pleading for rain. Look around, see the

drought. We haven't had rain in more than a year!' The fourth farmer just nods his head and tells them it's not going to work.

"The second farmer jumps in and says, 'We need the rain, we're putting our hearts into it, and we aren't asking for ourselves, but rather for our families and for our livestock.' The fourth farmer listens, nods, and says he still isn't impressed. 'You're just wasting time,' he says. The third farmer can't take any more, and in anger says, 'Okay, what would you do that we aren't doing?'

"The fourth farmer says, 'You really want to know?' The three other farmers say, 'We really want to know.'

"The fourth farmer says, 'I would've brought an umbrella!' "

There was a moment of silence between us. Irwin took a sip of Diet Snapple and waited for his words to sink in. "Larry, you have to *believe* the prayer will be answered."

"I'm still waiting for the proof."

"Proof of what, Larry? That God exists? That prayer works?"

"Yes."

"Think of the interviews as the evidence. You examine it. What does it tell you? What did you learn? What do you think?"

Once again there was that familiar silence between us. I polished off my bagel and Irwin sipped his Diet Snapple.

Then I said, "I just don't know, Irwin."

Irwin smiled. He knew that was coming. Then he looked down Broadway towards Times Square, taking it all in — the beauty of a bustling city.

Finally he said, "You know what, Larry? I'm hungry. I've been hungry ever since we started this trek. What do you say we go to Kosher Delight for a real breakfast?"

"Irwin, I just had a bagel."

The rabbi nodded and extended his hand to me. I took it, shook it, and said, "So that's it. You're finally giving up on me."

"I can't give up on you, Larry, I'm a rabbi. But right now I'm starving. I can't make you pray, Larry. Nobody can do that. The answer's right in front of you. It's right inside you. But it's something you have to want to find. I can only point the way. In the end, you must take the final steps of the journey alone."

Irwin threw his empty Snapple bottle into a nearby trashcan, clasped me on both shoulders, and looked deep into my eyes. For a minute, I was afraid he was going to kiss me, but he just said very earnestly, "Make a difference, Larry. Participate, don't coast. Take a moment to listen and you'll hear the words."

And then he put his finger just under his nose, at the little indentation right above his upper lip, and shushed me. He quickly turned and walked away.

I watched his black yarmulke disappear into

the morning crowd. When I could see him no longer, I headed in the opposite direction, toward Central Park South. As I crossed the street it occurred to me that I didn't have to be anywhere for another hour, so I decided to meander.

Not only is New York the greatest bagel city in the world, it is also one of the great walking cities. Today I made a point of looking at the city with fresh eyes, listening to the sounds of the street and smelling the fresh spring air.

At Columbus Circle, waiting to cross into Central Park, I remember saying quietly, "Thank you." I suppose it was for the blessings of being alive, finally having a fabulous wife, feeling wonderful, being surrounded by a vibrant, vital city — all of that.

I can't honestly say to whom that "thank you" was directed, but I know I wasn't talking to myself.

Epilogue

It was six o'clock in the morning and I was wide awake in my hotel room. Rabbi Katsof's words about listening had stayed with me all day. I was sitting in my chair in the living room, trying to puzzle it out.

I looked at The Schedule in my lap, hoping its familiarity would take my mind off the apprehension I was feeling. The coming day had a list of events and times and phone numbers two-pages long, but none of it was connecting. Something had changed and I didn't know what it was. I got out of the chair, leaving The Schedule behind, and walked to my window overlooking Central Park.

The morning light was just beginning to graze the treetops and I wondered if Pete Seeger was seeing the same thing miles away to the north and still singing the words of Mahalia Jackson, "I've seen God — I've seen the sunrise."

There it was, as the rabbi said, right in front of me and right inside me. I just started talking, albeit quietly. I was saying words and I didn't have a clue where they were going to take me.

"I'm not sure what I'm doing and I'm not

sure who I'm talking to. I don't need anything. I have a wife I love, a daughter I love, and a job I love. I'm helping people in my charity, so these words have no urgency. I mean, I'm sure there are others who need you more than I do right now, so if I'm *just* talking to this window because you have other issues, that's okay. And if I'm just talking to this window, that's okay too."

As a prayer it probably needed a little polishing, but then so did my hotel window. I guess we all could use a little polishing — maybe that's what a prayer does for the soul. I kept watching the sun rise in the east and thought of the many people who told me that a prayer is for the person praying, not for whatever or whomever they are praying to. But, of course, this wasn't a prayer at all. This was just a conversation.

"Anyway, I just want to say thank you during this quiet time rather than saying it down there with all the noise on the street. Might be easier to hear it from here."

This was starting to feel better as I plodded along. Then it struck me. This was the window the rabbi looked out so many months ago and told me somebody down there was saying a prayer. That idea didn't seem so foreign to me now.

I looked out at the dawn again. "One more issue," I said quietly, and then I took a deep breath. The sun was in full light over Central

Park now, but I had one more question. It came from that little boy in Brooklyn.

"What's this thing you have with the Yankees?"

Love thy neighbor as thyself.

Co-Author's Acknowledgments

First, I would like to thank Larry for letting me join him on this journey of understanding. I am deeply indebted to him for the opportunity to participate in this book and share my thoughts on prayer.

I would also like to thank my teacher, Rabbi Noah Weinberg, founder and dean of Aish HaTorah, who reconnected me with my heritage and spiritual roots. He taught me the importance of bringing God into my life and the absolute necessity of nurturing my spiritual self. Above all, he taught me I could converse with the Creator of the Universe, not just every day, but every moment of every day. The wisdom I share with you, the reader, I learned from him.

To my brother-in-law Rabbi Tom Meyer, and to Rabbi Motty Berger, Rabbi Michal Twersky, and Rabbi Zecharia Greiniman, of blessed memory, who taught me so much and guided me on my spiritual journey at so many critical junctures. I would have lost my way were it not for their lanterns.

To my colleagues Rabbi Nachum Braverman, Richard Horowitz, Richard Rabinowitz, Rabbi

Steve Baars, Rabbi Eric Coopersmith, Uriella Obst, and the rest of the terrific staff of Aish HaTorah International, thank you. You are an incredible team and the most dedicated group of individuals that anyone could ever ask to work with.

To Leibel Rudolph, taken from us at fifty-two years old, who was my partner for two intense years. The memory of your enthusiasm and unceasing quest to bring God into your life continues to inspire me.

To my father, who died this year after a short illness, and my mother, who was taken from us after a lengthy illness four years ago. Mom and Dad, I pray for you constantly. Your suffering and your deaths were the most difficult points in my relationship with God. I grew a lot and now feel closer to God, but I miss you both terribly. I wish you were here now to share this exciting experience with me. Thank you for giving me life and instilling in me the need to search for truth.

To my wife, Judy — you are the answer to my prayers, to what I was wise enough to ask for and to what I wasn't smart enough to ask for. You are a wellspring of inspiration and guidance. Thank you for being my partner. Thank you for your constant support. All my accomplishments are yours.

To our seven precious children — Batya, Aaron, Yaakov, Simcha, Bracha, Shalom, and Sara — you are each a gift from the Almighty and bring me immeasurable joy. Thank you, God!

May the Almighty grant us and our children the wisdom to live our lives to the utmost and may he bless us with good health, wisdom, and happiness.

Rabbi Irwin Katsof

If you have an interesting prayer story you would like to share or if you would like to bring the seminar "How to Get Your Prayers Answered" to your community or organization, please contact Rabbi Katsof at:

Phone: 1-212-713-0300
Fax: 1-212-713-0430
E-Mail: Myprayers@aol.com
Address: 156 West 56th Street, Suite 1201,
          New York, NY 10019

Index

Abdul-Jabbar, Kareem, 242–243
Adelson, Merv, 193–196
Alexander, Lamar, 271–272
Ali, Amir, 45–47
Ali, Muhammad, 246–248
Anderson, Jon, 203–206
Augustine, Norman, 198–200
Burke, Delta, 82–83
Bush, Barbara, 112
Carter, Jimmy, 107–112
Chopra, Deepak, 172–176
Cohen, Ben, 209–210
Colson, Chuck, 144–148, 324
Crosby, David, 73, 132–137
Dalai Lama, 60–61
Davis, Eric, 225–228
de Laurentiis, Dino, 207–208
De Angelis, Barbara, 318–320
Dershowitz, Alan, 127–130, 306–307
Dismore, Mark, 240–242
Dodd, Christopher, 260–263
Dossey, Larry, 157–160, 166–167
Douglas, Kirk, 68–71
Falwell, Rev. Jerry, 43–45, 255–256
Farrow, Mia, 123–125

Fishburne, Laurence, 75–76
Ford, Gerald, 106–107
Gould, Elliott, 89–90
Gray, John, 24, 313–315
Greenberg, Ace, 201
Greenfield, Jerry, 209–210
Haig, Alexander, 266–267, 287–290
Hamilton, Scott, 178–181
Hansen, Mark Victor, 327
Harris, Virginia, 167–172, 324–325, 328–329
Harron, Rev. Frank, 277
Hatch, Orrin, 176–178, 263–265
Hawn, Goldie, 98–100
Henderson, Florence, 31–32, 95–96
Hier, Rabbi Marvin, 48–51, 305–306
Holtz, Lou, 25–26, 230, 234–236
Huzienga, Wayne, 212–213
Jenner, Bruce, 231–233, 303–305
Keenan, Father Paul, 57–60
Kemp, Jack, 272–273
Kevorkian, Jack, 185–188
King, Alan, 87–89
Kirkpatrick, Jeane, 30–31, 265–266
Koch, Ed, 181–182
Kragen, Ken, 78
Lasorda, Tommy, 222–225
Leif, Judy, 62–63
Lowe, Peter, 315–317
Mann, Rev. Stephen, 163–165
Marriott, J. W., 210–212
Matthews, Dale, 161–163
McCain, John, 258–259, 290–294

Medved, Michael, 307–308
Murray, Rev. Cecil, 150–151
Nelson, Willie, 73–74
Peres, Shimon, 113–118
Phillips, Lou Diamond, 96–98, 302–303
Prager, Dennis, 320
Reed, Ralph, 251–255
Richards, Ann, 148–149, 327–328
Robbins, Anthony, 138–141, 320
Robbins, Tom, 83–86, 137–138
Rogers, Kenny, 77–78, 184–185, 309–310
Russo, Rene, 93–94
Sacks, David, 32–33, 201–203, 317–318
Schlessinger, Laura, 310–312
Schuller, Rev. Robert, 9–10, 64–65, 267–270
Schultz, Howard, 208–209
Scruggs, Jan, 280–283, 294–296
Seagal, Steven, 91–92
Seeger, Pete, 22–23, 71–72
Somers, Suzanne, 125–127
Spelling, Aaron, 325–326
Steiger, Rod, 81–82
Sweeney, Charles, 284–286
Templeton, Sir John Marks, 196–198
Thomas, Cal, 41–43, 142–144, 256, 326–327
Twerski, Abraham, 28–29, 188–189
Williamson, Marianne, 52–57
Wyle, Noah, 90, 183–184
Young, Steve, 237–240